SOVEREIGN LIVING III
A WOMAN'S GUIDE TO RECLAIMING YOUR
COMPASS

LAURA ALFANO

Sovereign Living III
A Woman's Guide to Reclaiming Your Compass

Laura Alfano

Copyright © 2026 Laura Alfano
All rights reserved

Laura Alfano
Alfano, Inc.
Malibu, California
LauraAlfano22@gmail.com
LauraAlfano.com

No part of this publication may be reproduced, distributed or transmitted in any form or by any means, including photocopying, recording, or other electronic or mechanical methods, without the prior written permission of the publisher, except in the case of brief quotations embodied in critical reviews and certain other noncommercial uses permitted by copyright law.

For permission requests, sales to U.S. bookstores and wholesalers, or to inquire about quantity discounts, please contact the publisher at the email address above.

Library of Congress Control Number: 2025923709

ISBN – 979-8-9938449-2-3

First Edition
10 9 8 7 6 5 4 3 2 1

Printed in the United States of America

SOVEREIGN LIVING III
A WOMAN'S GUIDE TO RECLAIMING YOUR
COMPASS

DEDICATION

This book is dedicated to my
three beautiful children and
their children, to my endlessly
patient parents, to my irreplaceable
siblings, and Alfano, Inc. You are all
a vital part of the legacy of love
that lives in these pages.

CONTENT

Part One - COMMUNICATIONS 1

Translating Emotions to Words 3
Compulsive Responses to Active Listening 9
Small Talk to Meaningful Conversation 15
Commiserating to an Empathetic Ear 21
Insecure to Confident 27
Deep Dirty Lies to White Hot Truth...........33
Preaching to Teaching 39
Speak to Be Heard...........................45

Part Two - BUSINESS.................51

Influence to Affluence........................53
Support Others to Yield Your Success 59
Hustle to Grace 65
Problems to Solutions........................71
Failure to Growth 77
Technology to Connectivity...................83
Endings to Beginnings 89
Random Relations to a Refined Sphere of
Influence...................................95
Most Important to Most Respected &
Influential.................................101
White Space to Closing the Gap 107
Fixed Mindset to Growth Mindset............113

Part Three - HOME 119
   Home to Sacred Space 121
   Selling a Home to Selling an Investment....... 129
   Selling One Investment to Unlock a
   Greater One 135
   Asset to 1031 Exchange 141
   Renting to Buying 147
   Land to Legacy 155

Part Four - ETIQUETTE 163
   Arriving Late to Being Early 165
   Unprepared to Prepared 171
   Disciplined to Devotional 177
   Buying a Gift to Thoughtful Gift Giving 183
   Text or Email to Handwritten Note 189
   Sorry to Excuse Me 195
   Apology to Appreciation 201
   Eating to Dining 207

AUTHOR'S NOTE

Dearest Reader,

Sovereign Living is an invitation to return home to yourself. It is not about perfection or performance but about alignment, living in harmony with your truth, your boundaries, and your deepest values. This book will help you recognize where you have given away your power and show you how to reclaim it with grace, clarity, and confidence.

This is more than a story; it is a lifeline. It shares my real and raw journey through life's firestorms, sometimes running, often walking, and in certain seasons, crawling, but always moving forward. These lessons were not learned in comfort; they were earned through heartbreak, courage, and perseverance. Each one became a stepping stone toward Sovereignty, and they can become yours too.

As you turn each page, let my voice steady you and my story remind you that you are not alone. I have been where you are and perhaps where you dare to go. I am here to guide you, believe in you, and walk this path with you.

A Call to Reclaim Your Sovereignty

For a woman, ***Sovereign Living*** is about unlearning dependence, reclaiming power, and defining life through her own inner authority rather than societal expectation. You were born Sovereign; it is your birthright.

This series of three books is a call to reclaim your Sovereignty: ***your Crown, your Heart, and your***

Compass. It reminds you that you are the ultimate authority in your life and invites you to rise in your own dominion. Each chapter offers a new perspective to help you move from self-doubt to self-mastery, from external validation to inner peace, and from autopilot to intention.

Sovereign Living invites you to step fully into your power and become the creator of your own life. Here, you will stand rooted in your truth, make decisions aligned with your soul, and create boundaries that honor your energy and well-being. You will be called to release outdated beliefs, shed conditioning, and let go of the need for approval. Instead, you will learn to trust your intuition, honor your desires, and take bold steps toward the life you deserve.

What Is Sovereign Living?

At its core, ***Sovereign Living*** is about embodying self-governance in every aspect of your life: emotional, spiritual, physical, and mental. It means standing firm in your values and beliefs, regardless of external expectations.

It is cultivating confidence and grace through every challenge and realizing that peace and happiness are not given by others but found within the deep well of wisdom and love already living inside you.

Sovereignty means living in alignment, connected to your truth, your purpose, and your deepest desires. It is not about power over others but about self-mastery and freedom from external validation. It is recognizing your worth, embracing your potential, and allowing yourself to thrive.

How to Use This Book

This book is meant to meet you where you are. You can read it from beginning to end or open to a chapter that speaks to your current experience. There are four parts organized by theme, and each stand on its own. One chapter a day may be all you have time for, and that is enough. You will receive what you need, exactly when you need it.

Each chapter of **Sovereign Living** is designed to guide your transformation. Consider this book a trusted companion on your journey, a way to awaken the Sovereign self within.

By way of my stories, self-inquiry exercises (*Reflect / Reframe / Reconnect*), journaling prompts, and mindful practices, you will uncover truths buried beneath layers of doubt, fear, and confusion. These practices are not meant to change who you are but to help you remember who you have always been.

Through the wisdom and insights shared in **Sovereign Living III: A Woman's Guide to Reclaiming Your Compass**, you will learn to navigate your outer world with clarity, purpose, and intention. This volume centers on alignment, how you express, create, and move through the spaces that define your daily life.

Part One: Communications invites you to speak with authenticity and listen with presence, cultivating relationships built on respect, truth, and understanding.

Part Two: Business encourages you to lead and create from integrity, balancing ambition with alignment, and redefining success on your own terms.

Part Three: Home explores the art of sanctuary, creating spaces that nurture peace, reflect your values, and support your evolution.

Part Four: Etiquette reimagines grace and mindfulness as modern forms of self-respect, reminding you that elegance begins with awareness and intention.

Together, these parts help you reclaim your inner compass, guiding you to live, lead, and communicate from the grounded wisdom of your Sovereign self.

Why Sovereignty Matters

In a world that feels chaotic and uncertain, Sovereignty is the foundation of peace. It is the grounding force that allows you to live with authenticity and freedom.

No matter where you are in your journey, this book will help you release the barriers that have kept you from stepping into your full potential. You do not need permission to be your most confident, authentic, and powerful self. You were born to lead your life with intention, courage, and clarity.

Everything you need already exists within you.

As Glinda said to Dorothy in *The Wizard of Oz*, "You have always had the power, my dear; you just had to learn it for yourself."

This is your time to live Sovereign, to stand in your truth, to step into your power, and to become the woman you were always meant to be.

Welcome to **Sovereign Living**, a journey back to yourself.

Let's get started,

Laura

INTRODUCTION

Sovereign [sov-rin]
   1. a monarch; a supreme ruler.
   Related Words: **absolute, autonomous, unlimited, self-governing, clear, true**

The dictionary defines *Sovereign* as power, as rule. But today, we expand its meaning from authority over others to mastery of self.

A **Sovereign Woman** is not led by circumstance; she is guided by her Compass, her inner truth, her steady north, her unwavering sense of direction in an ever-shifting world.

A **Sovereign Woman** is the keeper of her clarity, she moves with intention, speaks with integrity, and acts with alignment. She no longer drifts in reaction; she navigates with discernment.

A **Sovereign Woman** trusts her intuition as her instrument, listening not for approval, but for resonance.

A **Sovereign Woman** communicates with precision and presence, translating emotion into understanding, silence into wisdom, and truth into connection.

A **Sovereign Woman** leads with balance, bringing grace into business, purpose into prosperity, and authenticity into influence.

A **Sovereign Woman** cultivates her home as her foundation, creating sacred spaces that mirror her values and support her expansion.

A **Sovereign Woman** lives with elegance and respect, practicing modern etiquette not as performance, but as mindfulness in motion.

Above all, a **Sovereign Woman** is guided, not driven. Her Compass points inward before it points forward.

Can you feel that Compass within you, the quiet pull toward alignment, clarity, and confidence? Even when life feels uncertain, your inner guidance has never been lost. It has only been waiting beneath the noise of comparison, the chaos of expectation, and the fatigue of doing instead of being.

This book is written to help you return to it.

> *Sovereign Living* means reclaiming your true north, the inner guidance that directs every choice, conversation, and creation.
>
> *Sovereign Living* means mastering communication; speaking from truth rather than reaction, listening to understand rather than to win, and using words that heal rather than harm.
>
> *Sovereign Living* means approaching business with both intuition and integrity, turning ambition into alignment, and influence into impact.
>
> *Sovereign Living* means shaping your home as a sanctuary of energy and intention as well as a place where your environment nourishes your evolution.
>
> *Sovereign Living* means practicing etiquette as sacred grace; the art of presence, timing, and emotional intelligence that elevates every interaction.
>
> *Sovereign Living* is the art of navigation and orienting your outer world to reflect your inner truth. It is how you move through life not as a passenger of circumstance, but as the conscious captain of your own becoming.

Each chapter in *Sovereign Living III: A Woman's Guide to Reclaiming Your Compass* offers direction, reflection, and practical pathways to help you find your center and move forward with certainty. These are not rules to follow. They are coordinates to remember, guiding you home to yourself.

Because the **Sovereign Woman** doesn't chase direction, she *is* the direction. She lives by her Compass: calm, clear, and unshakably aligned.

Part One

COMMUNICATIONS
SPEAK FROM THE HEART WITH INTENTION, INTEGRITY & IMPACT

Communication is not just about words, it's about energy, intention, and alignment. The way we speak reveals the way we see ourselves. To reclaim your Compass begins with reclaiming your voice and to speak truthfully, lovingly, and with grounded authority.

In **Translating Emotions to Words**, you learn to speak from clarity and intention to shape your reality. **Compulsive Responses to Active Listening** invites you to pause before reacting, creating space for wisdom to enter the conversation. **Small Talk to Meaningful Conversation** transforms surface chatter into soulful exchange, where connection replaces performance.

In **Commiserating to an Empathetic Ear**, you shift from mirroring pain to holding presence, allowing compassion to become your language. **Insecure to Confident** reclaims the power of self-assured communication, where your words match your worth. **Deep Dirty Lies to White Hot Truth** asks for radical honesty, with yourself first. And **Preaching to Teaching** refines influence into grace: you stop convincing and start inspiring.

Finally, **Speak to Be Heard** reminds you that clarity is not volume, it's vibration. True communication isn't about being right; it's about being real. To speak Sovereignly is to let your words become bridges from head to heart, and from self to soul.

When communication becomes conscious, it transforms every interaction into an act of creation. Words no longer divide; they unite. They become instruments of truth, carriers of peace, and reflections of the love and clarity within. To speak with awareness is to live with integrity and to let every conversation become a mirror of your highest self.

TRANSLATING EMOTIONS TO WORDS

"Be impeccable with your word."
~ Don Miguel Ruiz

In *The Four Agreements*, Don Miguel Ruiz writes that your word is your power, a force of creation that shapes your reality. Of all his agreements, this one is the most essential: Be impeccable with your word.

Words are not just sounds. They're spells. They shape relationships, direct outcomes, and anchor your beliefs in the physical world. When spoken with clarity and intention, they have the power to align your inner and outer worlds.

But impeccability isn't just about honesty, it's about energy. Every word carries vibration. When you speak with integrity, your words become magnetic, drawing into form what your heart believes to be true. When you speak with doubt or fear, that same energy echoes back.

The voice is an instrument of manifestation and your tone, your truth, your timing, all become part of how life responds to you. Speaking with awareness is how you steer your inner guidance toward peace, purpose, and possibility. Your Soul naturally leans toward the experiences that hold your next evolution. Trust that instinct, it is your Compass home.

My Story: Speak It, Then See It

I live by a simple mantra that's become a quiet ritual: "Everything always works out for me." I repeat it in small, daily moments whether I'm rushing to an appointment, walking into a full restaurant without a reservation or navigating a client negotiation. And the results? Eight times out of ten, doors open. And the other two? I trust something better is on its way.

Words matter. Not just in what we say to others, but in how we speak to ourselves. When I affirm my reality with intention, things shift. When I speak from fear, things stall.

Over time, I've learned that when conversations feel heavy or misaligned, the most powerful question isn't, "Why don't they understand me?" It's this: "Am I being clear, calm, and consistent in both my words and my actions?" Because when I am, even the hardest truths have a way of landing with grace.

Speaking from Alignment, Not Emotion.

Your words are not just communication, they are creation. When your emotions and language are in harmony, you become a force for clarity, healing, and change. But when you speak from fear, reaction, or unresolved pain, words can become weapons.

This chapter invites you to pause, ground, and speak from a place of presence so your words reflect not just how you feel, but who you truly are.

Reflect

Reflection invites you to examine the language you regularly use, especially during stress or uncertainty. Words shape reality, and what you repeat, to yourself or others, becomes a script you live by. The goal is not to police your language but to become conscious of it. Are your words reinforcing fear or reinforcing trust?

- What phrases or internal scripts do you frequently say about yourself or your life, even if only in your thoughts?
- In moments of conflict or tension, do you respond with clarity, or react from fear or defensiveness?
- Consider the recent impact of your words. Have they built trust, or created distance and misunderstanding?

Journaling Prompt: *What patterns do I notice in my language and how do they reflect what I believe about myself or others?*

Reframe

Reframing invites you to speak as someone who is already aligned with their truth and values. Your words are not just tools, they are extensions of your emotional state. When you shift your inner dialogue, your outer communication becomes more compassionate, consistent, and impactful.

- Your words carry energy. When you speak with self-respect, others are invited to meet you there.
- Miscommunication is often a result of emotional misalignment, not just poor wording.
- You model how others should listen to you by how consistently you speak from calm truth, not charged reaction.

Mantra: *When I speak from clarity, I shape my world with intention and peace.*

Reconnect

Reconnection is the practice of aligning your inner state with your outer expression. It means bringing mindfulness to your words, especially when emotions run high. Integrity is not built by avoiding reactivity, but by choosing to respond with presence, clarity, and a steady commitment to your values.

- **Anchor in Daily Affirmation**
  Begin each day with a grounding phrase. Try: "Everything always works out for me." Let this shape your tone and outlook.

- **Ask Before Speaking**
  Check in with yourself:
  – "What's my intention?"
  – "What tone is needed here?"
  – "Am I being honest and kind?"

- **Pause When Emotions Run High**
  When triggered, don't rush to speak. Take a breath. Let your values lead, not your wounds.

Affirmation: *My words reflect my wisdom. I speak with clarity, compassion, and grounded truth.*

Final Thought: Let Your Words Become Your Wand

Words are not just tools.
They are living energy.
Every syllable carries intention.
Every truth spoken shapes reality.

When your inner voice and outer words align,
you move in integrity.
You speak light into form.
You call peace into motion.

Speak with care.
Speak with clarity.
Speak with love.

Let your words uplift,
not undo.
Let silence serve as wisdom,
and speech as devotion.

Be the woman whose word is gold,
whose voice leads with grace.

This is Sovereign Living.

COMPULSIVE RESPONSES TO ACTIVE LISTENING

*"Most people do not listen with
the intent to understand; they listen
with the intent to reply."*
~ Stephen R. Covey

We are biologically wired for efficiency making thousands of decisions and processing countless thoughts each day. But this mental autopilot can cost us the most vital part of human connection: the ability to truly listen.

> Most people aren't listening. They're waiting.
> Waiting to speak, defend, or be right.
> Waiting to fix what doesn't need fixing.
> Waiting to protect their own narrative.

This habit, often unconscious, creates distance in our most important relationships at work, at home, and especially in love. When we listen only through the filter of our own story, we stop hearing the truth in someone else's. We stop meeting the heart that's trying to reach us.

Active listening breaks that cycle. It allows us to be present, receptive, and responsive, not reactive. It invites humility, curiosity, and patience, the quiet virtues of emotional intelligence. Active listening doesn't just improve communication; it heals misunderstanding before words even form. It shifts conversation from surface to soul, from noise to meaning.

My Story: Presence Builds Lasting Trust

As a real estate agent, active listening is not just a skill; it is a daily discipline. I give every client the same focused attention, beginning with a simple but powerful gesture: I silence my phone and keep it out of sight. When I am fully present, so are they.

I listen closely to their needs and desires, all while painting a mental picture of the home they are searching for. I begin with the essentials; their nonnegotiables and must-haves and then I ask thoughtful, specific questions:

- What is your top-end budget?
- How many bedrooms and bathrooms do you need?
- Do you envision yourself on the beach, or perched on a hill with ocean views?

As they respond, I visualize each detail. The conversation becomes a co-creative process where every answer brings clarity and narrows the possibilities. This intentional listening allows me not only to align with their vision but also to gently eliminate options that will not serve them.

When the buyers are a couple, I am mindful that each person brings their own vision. It is essential to communicate with both at once, so they can hear and understand each other's priorities. My role is not to persuade one over the other; it is to bring alignment. I help surface common ground, highlight differences with care, and ensure both partners feel seen and heard. This builds not just consensus but trust, a trust that extends well beyond the transaction.

When trust is present, clients turn to you not only for homes but for life. They ask for referrals to contractors, movers, landscapers, and cleaning services. For those new to the area, they seek your insight on local restaurants, weekend activities, and ways to entertain visiting friends and family. Because when people know you are truly listening, they know you truly care.

The Gift of True Presence

Listening isn't about waiting for your turn to speak, it's about creating space where others feel seen, safe, and valued. In a world that often rushes to solve, fix, or defend, the rarest and most healing offering is your full, quiet attention.

When you shift from listening to respond toward listening to understand, you transform communication into connection. When you listen with your heart as much as your ears, you give others permission to do the same. True listening is love in motion, the kind that turns noise into harmony, and strangers into trust.

Reflect

Reflection allows you to get honest about your listening habits. Are you really hearing people, or simply preparing your reply? Listening isn't just about hearing words; it's about reading the emotion underneath, honoring the silence between them, and offering presence without trying to control the outcome.

- Ask yourself: "Do I listen to respond, fix, or prove a point or do I listen to truly understand?"

- Reflect on the last time you felt deeply heard. What made that moment feel safe and impactful?
- Consider any relationships where you tend to interrupt, talk over, or shut down others unintentionally. What drives that reaction?

Journaling Prompt: *What gets in the way of me fully listening and what might shift if I prioritized presence over performance?*

Reframe

Reframing helps you redefine listening as a sacred exchange, not a transaction. You don't have to fix people's pain to support them. Often, what others most need is the gift of being seen without judgment, advice, or redirection. Presence is not passive, it's powerful.

- Listening is a generous act. You're not there to perform wisdom, but to create space for others to feel heard.
- You don't need to offer solutions. Sometimes being a soft place to land is the highest form of service.
- Silence isn't something to rush through, it's often where truth begins to emerge.

Mantra: *I create space for others to feel heard, not hurried.*

Reconnect

Reconnection turns conscious listening into a daily practice of relational integrity. It's about tuning in fully with your body, energy, and attention. When people feel truly heard, healing happens. When you listen deeply, trust is built through presence, not through clever words.

- **Engage with Full Attention**
  Make eye contact. Turn your body toward the speaker. Set your phone aside. Let your presence speak before your words do.

- **Ask Before You Offer**
  Before giving advice, ask: "Would you like support, or just someone to listen?" Let them guide the exchange.

- **Practice Reflective Listening**
  Mirror what you hear. Try: "It sounds like you're saying…" or "What I'm hearing is…" This shows care, not control.

- **Choose Real-Time Connection**
  When emotions run high, opt for voice or face-to-face communication instead of text. Tone and presence matter.

Affirmation: *I listen with intention, offer presence over performance, and honor connection above control.*

Final Thought: Listen to Understand, Not to Respond

Listening is not silence.
It is presence.
It is the art of softening so another can unfold.

Pause the urge to fix.
Quiet the need to be right.
Let words land before they pass through you.

Be the mirror, not the megaphone.
Reflect, don't react.
Hold space for truth to rise on its own timing.

In a world of noise, listening is power.
It builds trust without effort,
influence without control,
connection without demand.

When you can sit in another's story
without rushing to rescue or repair,
you offer the rarest gift, safety.

This is leadership.
This is love.

This is Sovereign Living.

SMALL TALK TO MEANINGFUL CONVERSATION

"You are here to enrich the world, and you impoverish yourself if you forget the errand."
~ Woodrow Wilson

There is nothing more draining than surface-level small talk, the kind that circles around traffic, weather, or worn-out complaints. It may fill the silence, but it rarely fills the soul. True connection requires more: presence, intention, and curiosity.

Whether meeting someone for the first time or reconnecting with someone you have known for decades, there is always a choice: keep it light or go a little deeper. Most people are quietly longing for more; they are simply waiting for permission.

Meaningful conversation acts like a Compass. It orients you toward authenticity, toward what truly matters. When we speak from curiosity rather than habit, we stop drifting in circles and begin finding direction. Each honest exchange becomes a subtle course correction, guiding us closer to purpose, belonging, and truth.

To converse with presence is to honor the sacred in another person. It transforms dialogue into discovery and words into bridges of understanding. Sovereign communication is not about saying more; it is about saying what is real. When we speak with awareness, we do more than connect; we create resonance, and that resonance becomes love in motion.

My Story: Beyond Titles, Into Truth

I've never loved cocktail-party conversations. You know the type: "So, what do you do?" followed by a mental filing of your answer into a neat little box, status, success and worth. I played that game for years. Smiled politely. Answered predictably. Walked away feeling hollow.

Now, I lead differently. When I meet someone, I don't ask what they do, I ask what they love. I ask what excites them, what's lighting them up, what they'd be doing if time and money weren't in the way.

I've found that one question, when asked with real interest, can crack someone open. You'll see it in their face. A softening. A spark. A drop in the shoulders, like they've finally been invited to take off their armor. One story that still moves me began in real estate but turned into something much bigger.

I was helping a young couple begin their search for buying their first home. They were diligent, practical, and focused on every dollar. But when we sat with my mortgage broker, the conversation shifted.

The couple revealed that, while they worked in tech, their true passion was social impact and building platforms to track and amplify good in the world. That lit something up in my mortgage broker, whose son designs bespoke experiences for high-net-worth clients: private travel, impossible-to-get concert tickets, and once-in-a-lifetime moments. And that reminded me of my youngest daughter, who curates intimate and large scale, elevated events. Her greatest joy is experienced when the activations serve a greater good, like Foster Love fundraisers, and nonprofit galas.

I didn't want those threads of connection to disappear. So I invited everyone to a dinner. We were different generations, industries and backgrounds yet by dessert, we were talking about legacy, purpose, and impact. Not because anyone tried to be deep, but because everyone was open.

That meal reminded me: every person contains a spark of something meaningful. If you're brave enough to ask the right question, and quiet enough to really listen, you'll find it.

Cultivating Meaningful Conversation Through Intentional Dialogue

Meaningful conversation doesn't just happen, it's cultivated through presence, curiosity, and care. When you shift from surface-level exchanges to soul-centered dialogue, you create space for both yourself and others to feel seen.

Connection is not about always going deep, it's about creating the safety and sincerity that make depth possible. The more you practice intentional conversation, the more you strengthen your inner Compass, learning not only how to guide others, but how to guide yourself back to what truly matters.

Reflect

Reflection invites you to examine how you currently engage in conversation. Are you seeking connection, or validation? Do your daily interactions fill you up or leave you feeling unseen? When you pause to evaluate your role in dialogue, you begin to shift the energy from transactional to transformational.

- When was the last time you walked away from a conversation feeling truly seen, heard, and understood?

- Consider whether you lead with curiosity or with the desire to be impressive. Which energy invites others in?

- Think about your most common conversations. Do they nourish your spirit or drain your energy?

Journaling Prompt: *What do my conversations say about what I value and what kind of connection I'm truly seeking?*

Reframe

Reframing helps you release the pressure to perform and invites you to focus on presence. Connection doesn't require cleverness, it requires sincerity. Every conversation doesn't have to be profound to be meaningful; sometimes, the simplest exchanges are the ones that open the deepest doors.

- Small talk can be sacred, it's not the final destination, but an opening to something more.

- You don't need to impress people to connect with them, you need to be real, receptive, and present.

- Depth unfolds in safe spaces. Create emotional safety first, and meaning will naturally follow.

Mantra: *I don't speak to be impressive. I speak to connect with honesty and heart.*

Reconnect

Reconnection is about turning presence into practice. Whether you're speaking to a loved one or a stranger, you have the ability to initiate depth through warmth and intention. Connection happens when we ask better questions, listen generously, and follow through with care.

- **Ask Heart-Opening Questions**
  Go beyond surface talk. Try:
  – "What's something you're looking forward to?"
  – "What's bringing you peace right now?"
  – "What's one thing that surprised you this year?"

- **Listen Generously**
  Don't just hear, receive. Listen without planning your reply. Let their words land.

- **Follow Up**
  When someone shares something meaningful, remember it. Circle back. Ask how it unfolded. This is how trust grows.

- **Name the Connection**
  If a moment feels meaningful, say so. A simple compliment such as, "I've really enjoyed this conversation" creates warmth and affirmation.

Affirmation: *I speak with presence, listen with care, and create conversations that nourish connection.*

Final Thought: Turn Conversation Into Connection

Small talk may start the exchange,
but soul talk builds the bridge.

You don't need a script; you need sincerity.
You don't need to impress; you need to care.

When you approach every conversation
with presence, purpose, and curiosity,
you create sacred space for someone to feel seen.

True dialogue is not performance, it's alignment.
It's the meeting of two inner Compasses,
each one guiding the other gently home.

Let your words be steady,
your silence be generous,
your attention be whole.

In doing so, you enrich your life
with what matters most: meaning, not metrics.

Depth doesn't require perfection,
it simply requires intention.

Ask. Listen. Witness. Share.
This is how we shift from surface to soul,
one conversation at a time.

This is Sovereign Living.

COMMISERATING TO AN EMPATHETIC EAR

"Misery loves company."
~John Ray

It's a natural instinct: when someone shares their pain, we reach for our own story in response. We want to comfort, relate, and prove we understand. But too often, that good intention becomes unintentional hijacking. The moment shifts from their experience to ours. And though it may seem like connection, what they may feel instead is interruption.

True empathy doesn't rush to relate. It resists the urge to match grief with grief. It simply says: "I'm here. Keep going."

Empathy is a Compass of the heart, it points us toward presence, not performance. It teaches us to orient ourselves around another's pain without losing our own center. In this balance, we discover that connection isn't about mirroring someone's suffering, it's about helping them find light within it.

My Story: Compassion Begins With True Presence

After my father passed away, I was surprised by how many people began sharing stories of losing their own dads. Some spoke of regrets, others of reconciliation. Many recounted favorite memories, some sweet, others searing.

At first, I felt disconnected. *Why are they making this about them?* I thought. I wasn't ready to compare pain.

I needed space to feel my own. But then I softened. I saw what was really happening. They weren't trying to take the moment, in fact, they were trying to meet me in it. It was their way of saying, *You're not alone.*

The lesson? Sometimes connection looks clumsy. Sometimes comfort sounds like storytelling. But underneath it all is a human trying to reach another.

Now, when someone is grieving, I hold back my own story unless invited. I resist the impulse to advise or relate. I let them lead. I follow gently. I ask, "What do you miss most?" or "What's something you're holding onto that still brings you peace?"

I've learned that the deepest form of compassion is not found in commiserating, but in listening with your whole heart. The kind of listening that doesn't rush to rescue, but rests beside the ache until it breathes on its own.

The Strength of Silent Support

Holding space means allowing someone to be fully seen and heard without needing to fix, compare, or shift the focus. In a world that often rushes to respond or relate, true presence is rare and powerful.

Empathy doesn't require words, it requires awareness. It's knowing when to speak, when to stay silent, and when to simply be there. This chapter is a call to practice the kind of listening that honors another's experience, not by taking the spotlight, but by standing quietly beside them with compassion, stillness, and grace.

Reflect

Reflection helps you become aware of your patterns in vulnerable conversations. Do you try to comfort others by inserting your own story? Do you rush to offer advice, even with good intentions? Holding space begins by noticing the moments when your need to relate might unintentionally overshadow someone else's need to be heard.

- When someone shares something vulnerable, do you instinctively respond with "I've been through that too"?
- Do you find silence uncomfortable and fill it with your own experiences or thoughts?
- Recall a time when someone truly listened to you witnot offering advice. What made that experience so powerful?

Journaling Prompt: *What changes when I listen to understand, instead of trying to relate or rescue?*

Reframe

Reframing invites you to view listening not as a passive role, but as an active and loving choice. Empathy is not about having the perfect words, it's about making space for someone else's truth. You don't need to fix their pain to be a part of their healing. Presence alone can be profound.

- Empathy isn't "I know exactly how you feel." It's "I'm with you, even if I don't fully understand."
- Listening is an act of humility, love, and deep respect.

- Holding space requires less speaking and more honoring of the silence, of the emotion, and of the timing.

Mantra: *My presence is enough. I hold space by honoring what needs to be felt, not fixed.*

Reconnect

Reconnection is the practice of letting your presence speak more loudly than your opinions. When someone opens up, give them the gift of full attention and emotional spaciousness. Holding space doesn't require the right response, it requires the right intention.

- **Pause Before You Respond**
  Let the other person lead. Resist the urge to fill silence. Let them fully express before you speak.

- **Use Gentle, Supportive Prompts Try:**
  – "Would it help to talk more about that?"
  – "What's felt the heaviest for you lately?"

- **Offer Nonverbal Support**
  A kind look. A soft nod. A steady presence. These subtle signals often say more than any words.

- **Respect Emotional Boundaries**
  You don't need to carry their pain, just sit beside it with care and without judgment.

Affirmation: *I hold space with presence, humility, and love. I don't need to fix. I only to witness with grace.*

Final Thought: Be the Space, Not the Spotlight

Empathy is not about echoing pain,
it's about making room for it.

When you resist the urge to insert your story,
you offer something sacred: space.

Space to be heard.
Space to be held.
Space to heal.

In that quiet, steady presence,
you become a sanctuary for someone else's truth.

You become the still point in another's storm,
the pause between their heartbreak and their breath.

Empathy doesn't shout, it steadies.
It reminds both souls: we are not alone here.

True compassion requires no spotlight,
only light.

This is Sovereign Living.

INSECURE TO CONFIDENT

"Confidence is silent. Insecurities are loud."
~ Don Corleone, The Godfather

Think of the people you admire. Do they walk into a room and do not need to say much to be felt? Does their presence do the talking? Is their energy steady, grounded, and self-assured? That is the essence of true confidence. It does not need to prove. It does not need to perform. It simply is.

We often mistake volume for strength, but noise is not power. Power is focus. Power is stillness. Power is clarity. Confidence is not found in how loudly you speak, but in how deeply you are anchored. It is the calm assurance that comes from knowing who you are and who you are not.

True confidence is built quietly, through integrity, consistency, and self-respect. It grows each time you keep a promise to yourself, each time you show up authentically, and each time you choose peace over performance. Confidence is not an attitude; it is alignment. It is the steady knowing that you do not need to take up more space to be powerful; you simply need to occupy your own with grace.

My Story: From Expression to Effective Influence

I grew up in a large Italian family and loved every minute of it. Sunday dinners were a full-sensory experience: elders speaking rapid-fire Italian, arms flailing, hands gesturing, eyes rolling, hips swaying. I came to believe that this was how you made a message land; with passion, volume, movement. It wasn't just communication; it was performance.

That expressive style became part of me. I carried it through my teenage years, into college, and into my early career. It served me well until one pivotal moment shifted everything.

I was 33, preparing for a high-stakes budget meeting with the VP of Sales and the VP of Marketing. At the time, I reported directly to the VP of Marketing, with a dotted line to the VP of Sales. We were launching a new hair care brand, and I was responsible for securing retail placement at CVS and Walgreens. The meeting's purpose was to secure critical funding from Marketing, so Sales could execute the launch and drive immediate distribution and sales velocity.

An hour before the meeting, the VP of Sales, also Italian, pulled me aside. Gently and respectfully, he said, "Can I offer you some advice? Sit on your hands while you talk. Slow your pace and make direct eye contact with the VP of Marketing."

He continued: "I understand you fully, your intent, enthusiasm, and creativity. But he's watching your hands more than hearing your message. The volume and movement are distracting him. He hears you, but he's not quite sure what you're asking for. Keep it simple. Be direct. You've got a solid case, just let that speak for itself."

I trusted Joe. I knew his background, and I knew he wanted what was best for all of us. I took his feedback to heart. In that meeting, I shifted my delivery: calm, clear, and composed. I stuck to the key points. And it worked. We got the full funding.

That moment taught me a lesson I've carried ever since: great communication isn't just about passion, it's about precision, presence, and knowing your audience. True power doesn't need to persuade; it simply stands in truth.

Speaking from Center, Not for Approval

Confidence is not volume, performance, or persuasion it's presence. When you speak from inner alignment, your words carry clarity and conviction without needing to convince. Real confidence feels like breath returning to your body. It feels steady, measured and whole. It's the energy of a woman who no longer chases validation because she's learned to validate herself.

This chapter guides you to recognize and release performative patterns, so you can express yourself with rooted confidence, not from the need to be seen, but from the truth that you already *are*.

Reflect

Reflection helps you become aware of the habits and insecurities that shape how you speak, especially in moments that matter most. Expressing confidently doesn't mean being the loudest in the room; it means being the most aligned. Begin by noticing when your communication shifts from authentic to performative.

- In high-stakes or vulnerable moments, do you find yourself rushing, over explaining, or overcompensating with gestures?

- Do you associate passion with volume or intensity and does that truly reflect your most grounded expression?
- Ask yourself honestly: "Am I seeking validation, or am I already standing in what I know to be true?"

Journaling Prompt: *What shifts in my body and voice when I speak from self-trust instead of seeking approval?*

Reframe

Reframing helps you redefine what confidence actually looks and feels like. It's not about dominating a room, it's about being fully at home in your body, message, and truth. True presence is magnetic because it's rooted in calm clarity, not performance or pretense.

- Confidence is not force, it's the quiet power of alignment and certainty.
- The most impactful voices speak not to be heard, but because they carry something meaningful.
- Presence is felt more in stillness than in spectacle. When you speak from your center, others naturally want to listen.

Mantra: *I don't perform to be seen. I speak because I have something true to share.*

Reconnect

Reconnection is the practice of anchoring your voice in your body and your values. Whether you're entering a conversation, a stage, or a difficult discussion, your energy communicates long before your words do. Speak not to impress, but to express clearly, calmly, and confidently.

- **Ground Yourself First**
  Before speaking, take a breath. Place your hand on your heart or belly. Feel your presence. Let your body settle into trust.

- **Speak from Belonging**
  Walk into every room as if you already belong, because you do. Let your energy reflect that truth.

- **Use Silence with Intention**
  Pause between points. Let your words land. Silence is not a gap, it's a tool for resonance.

- **Choose Clarity Over Cleverness**
  Say what you mean. Speak simply. Confidence doesn't need to decorate itself to be powerful.

- **Practice with Support**
  Record yourself. Speak with a trusted friend or mentor. Pay attention to how your energy shifts when you're grounded in truth.

Affirmation: *I express myself with clarity, calm, and confidence. I speak from truth, not for approval.*

Final Thought: Let Presence Speak Louder Than Performance

True confidence isn't loud; it's luminous.
It doesn't chase approval; it emanates assurance.

It doesn't fill space; it *anchors* it.
It doesn't dominate; it steadies.

Confidence is not found in volume,
but in the quiet rhythm of self-trust.

It's rooted in stillness.
In clarity.
In knowing who you are, without apology.

When you move from insecure performance
to embodied presence,
you stop trying to impress
and begin to *influence.*

The most magnetic person in the room
isn't the one who speaks the most,
but the one whose silence carries truth.

This is Sovereign Living

DEEP DIRTY LIES TO WHITE HOT TRUTH

"Truth is a journey."
~ Danielle LaPorte

Telling the truth is not just an act; it is a devotion, a sacred return to yourself. Yet for many of us, honesty becomes complicated. Somewhere along the way, we learn to edit, soften, or silence what is real. We lie, not to deceive, but to protect and to avoid conflict, shame, or disappointment.

We tell partial truths to keep the peace, smile through discomfort to preserve connection, or stay silent to avoid being labeled "too much." But every unspoken truth becomes emotional clutter, heavy and loud within the body. It takes energy to hide what aches to be revealed. The more we conceal, the more distant we become from our authentic selves.

The truth never disappears. It waits patiently beneath the surface, pressing up through discomfort and asking to be seen. Because without truth, nothing lasting can be built. Not relationships. Not careers. Not self-worth. To live Sovereignly is to walk in radical honesty, first with yourself and then with the world. Only when truth is spoken with grace does love, integrity, and peace begin to take root and flourish.

My Story: Self-Abandonment Disguised as Peace

The lie I told most in my marriage was small and only two words: "I'm fine." I said it often. And every time,

I buried a little more of myself. I used that phrase like armor to avoid confrontation, to preserve peace, and to hide my exhaustion or heartache.

But every "I'm fine" created distance. Distance from my husband. Distance from intimacy. Most dangerously, distance from my own truth. I began moving through the motions of marriage, smiling on the outside while shrinking on the inside. The silence felt safer than honesty, but it was slowly erasing me.

I did not speak up when I felt overwhelmed. I did not name it when I felt unseen. I did not trust that my feelings would be received with care. So I silenced them until the silence hardened into resentment, until I could no longer feel much of anything at all. That emotional disconnection became a chasm too wide to cross.

Looking back, I see it clearly: the lie was never protection. It was conflict avoidance, rooted in a pattern of self-abandonment. And truth, though harder in the moment, would have been the most loving act of all, a gift of freedom for both of us.

Healing Through Honest Expression

Truth is not just about facts, it's about freedom. When you communicate with honesty, you don't just clear the air; you create space for healing, clarity, and deeper connection. Avoiding the truth may feel easier in the moment, but it often leads to prolonged tension and misalignment. This chapter invites you to speak your truth not as a weapon, but as a path to wholeness for yourself and others.

Reflect

Reflection is the starting point for honest communication. Truth-telling begins by acknowledging what you've been avoiding in your conversations, your relationships, or within yourself. The fear of discomfort often keeps truth buried, but silence rarely protects us in the long run. It only delays what needs to be faced and felt.

- Identify the truths you're currently avoiding in your relationships, in your work, or within your own heart.
- Consider the subtle or spoken lies you've told to avoid tension or rejection.
- Ask yourself: "What have I been afraid might happen if I said what I really feel or believe?"

Journaling Prompt: *What truth have I been carrying and what would it feel like to finally release it with clarity and care?*

Reframe

Reframing allows you to see truth as a tool of compassion, not confrontation. Speaking honestly doesn't require volume or intensity, it requires clarity, alignment, and love. Your truth, expressed from a grounded place, has the power to liberate both you and those around you.

- Truth doesn't have to be loud, it simply needs to be clear and steady.
- Honesty, when delivered with love, is a gift, not a disruption.

- You can be both kind and direct. Delaying truth often deepens pain. Sharing it wisely can initiate healing.

Mantra: *My truth is not a threat. It is an offering of clarity, care, and connection.*

Reconnect

Reconnection is the practice of bringing your truth into the light, one small step at a time. It's about choosing honesty, not to win or dominate, but to align with your values and invite real connection. When you communicate with truth and love, you create an environment where healing becomes possible. Healing for you and for those ready to meet you in that space.

- **Practice Micro-Truths**
  Start small. Replace default responses like "I'm fine" with something more real: "I'm figuring it out" or "I'm feeling a bit off today."

- **Journal to Clarify Truth**
  Write daily to explore what you're feeling, what you've left unsaid, and what might need to be spoken with love.

- **Prepare for Difficult Conversations**
  Breathe. Ground yourself. Set an intention not to control, but to connect. Speak from your heart, even if your voice shakes.

- **Use Truth as a Tool of Healing**
  Speak honestly, but don't weaponize your words. Let truth be the bridge not the barrier.

- **Trust the Outcome**
  When you express your truth with compassion,

the people who are meant to walk with you will understand and stay.

Affirmation: *I speak truth with courage and compassion. My honesty heals, frees, and deepens connection.*

Final Thought: Speak the Truth That Sets You Free

You don't need to bulldoze.
You don't need to justify.
You only need to be honest, first with yourself, then with others.

Because every time you silence your truth to make someone else comfortable,
you abandon a piece of your soul.
And your soul deserves wholeness.

Truth isn't harsh, it's healing.
It's the light that dissolves confusion.
It's the Compass that guides you home.

Speak with love.
Speak with clarity.
Speak even when your voice trembles.
Because the life you long for depends on it.

The right people will rise to meet your honesty.
The wrong ones will fall away in peace.

And what remains will be real.

This is Sovereign Living.

PREACHING TO TEACHING

"The difference between preaching and teaching: one makes you feel good, the other makes you grow."
~ T.F. Hodge

There's a sacred difference between helping and fixing, as well as between offering truth and offering trust. Preaching may be well-intentioned, but it often centers the speaker. It delivers certainty, solution, and control, sometimes at the cost of empathy. It assumes we know what someone else needs, when in truth, we rarely do.

Teaching, in contrast, centers the other. It's less about telling someone what to do and more about creating the conditions for their own knowing to emerge. Teaching honors Sovereignty and it trusts that each person holds the wisdom they need, even if it's buried beneath confusion or fear.

Teaching is spacious. It listens more than it lectures. It honors timing, tenderness, and individual truth. It doesn't rush to be right. It invites someone inward to listen to themselves, trust themselves, and grow.

When we move from preaching to teaching, we move from ego to empathy, from directing someone's path to walking beside them in grace. That is where transformation truly begins.

My Story: Hold Space, Don't Fill It

I first understood the depth of this distinction at Modern Elder Academy in Baja, Mexico. During one afternoon workshop, a man in our group began to share. He was visibly stretched thin, now living in a new city, a demanding job, two young children, and an aging father-in-law whose health was failing thousands of miles away. His voice trembled with exhaustion and uncertainty.

I felt his pain in my body. My own experiences of caregiving, parenting and professional overwhelm surged to the surface. I wanted to help. I wanted to share what I'd learned the hard way. I opened my mouth to speak. But before I could finish my first sentence, he gently held up his hand. "I don't need advice," he said, his eyes soft. "I need help finding my own answers."

I sat back in my chair. And in that moment, everything shifted. He wasn't asking for my story. He was asking for my presence. He didn't want my path. He needed space to find his own.

That moment changed the way I support others forever. I learned that wisdom shared too soon can interrupt the sacred unfolding of another's truth and that real guidance often looks like quiet patience.

Guiding Without Grabbing the Reins

Support doesn't require leadership, it requires presence. In moments when others are vulnerable, the most meaningful act is not to fix or direct, but to hold space with patience and humility. When you resist the urge to take over, you empower others to access their own clarity, resilience, and wisdom. True support uplifts without overshadowing.

Reflect

Reflection helps you identify your tendencies when others turn to you for support. Do you rush to solve? Interrupt with advice? These patterns, often born from love or discomfort, can unintentionally take away someone's power. By slowing down and becoming aware, you open the door to deeper connection and more impactful support.

- Do you find yourself giving advice quickly, even before the person has fully shared?
- Have you ever felt unheard in a conversation, and what did that experience teach you?
- When others share something difficult, do you feel a need to solve it in order to be helpful or feel useful?

Journaling Prompt: *What shifts when I stop trying to lead and instead choose to witness and reflect?*

Reframe

Reframing invites you to let go of the pressure to have answers. You don't need to be the expert to be helpful, you just need to be available and attuned. Holding space is not passive; it's an active expression of trust in someone else's ability to find their way.

- Teaching doesn't mean having all the answers, it means walking beside someone, not in front of them.
- True listening creates more transformation than the best advice ever could.

- You don't need to carry their burden. Just your presence can help lighten it.

Mantra: *I don't need to fix. I need to witness with care and trust.*

Reconnect

Reconnection is the practice of supporting others by trusting their wisdom, not replacing it. This kind of support centers the other person, not your role in their story. When you create space for reflection rather than direction, you empower growth that's grounded in ownership and authenticity.

- **Ask Before Offering**
  Begin with: "Would it help to hear what's worked for me or do you just need space to be heard?"

- **Practice the Pause**
  When they finish speaking, pause for a full breath or two. Let silence hold the weight. Trust that you don't need to fill it.

- **Use Empowering Questions**
  – "What do you already know but might be afraid to act on?"
  – "What support would feel most nourishing right now?"

- **Reflect Their Strengths**
  Don't jump to answers, reflect what you hear with love. Remind them of their capacity. Let them lead their own way forward.

Affirmation: *I support others by creating space, not control. I trust their wisdom and honor their process.*

Final Thought: Teach with Questions, Not Conclusions

True teaching doesn't shout; it whispers.
It doesn't preach; it partners.
It meets others where they are.
Not where you wish them to be.

Presence leads more gently than pressure.
It reminds others their answers live within.
You become a mirror, not a map.
Reflection matters more than direction.

Real wisdom invites, never demands.
It asks questions instead of giving orders.
It trusts timing more than tactics.
It allows silence to do its work.

Teaching is an act of faith.
A belief that light finds its way.
Your calm becomes their compass.
Your belief in them helps them believe too.

This is Sovereign Living.

SPEAK TO BE HEARD

"People start to heal the moment they feel heard."
~ Cheryl Richardson

From a young age, many of us were taught that silence is safety. We were told to be polite, to avoid conflict, and to keep the peace at any cost. "Don't rock the boat." "If you can't say something nice, don't say anything at all." These phrases were meant to protect us, to help us belong. But over time, silence can become a cage. What once kept us safe can start to keep us small.

True peace is not the absence of conflict; it is the presence of truth spoken with care. When we withhold our words to avoid discomfort, we begin to fracture inside. The body remembers every moment we bite our tongue, every emotion we bury, every truth we silence. Avoidance may bring temporary calm, but it creates long-term disconnection from others, and most painfully, from ourselves.

Speaking up, kindly and clearly, is not confrontation. It is liberation. It is how we reclaim the parts of ourselves we once muted for acceptance. Every time you give voice to what is real, you create harmony between your inner world and your outer life. To speak is to honor your Sovereignty. To be heard is to begin to heal.

My Story: Reclaiming Truth, Releasing Silence

This truth came alive within me, quite literally, during a plant medicine ceremony at Rythmia Life

Advancement Center in Costa Rica. At the height of the experience, I felt a forceful cracking through my clavicle and rib cage, followed by a surge of energy that spiraled down through my throat and into my heart. The sound and sensation were real, yet there was no fear. A deep calm filled me as I understood something sacred was being released.

The next morning, a shaman confirmed what I already sensed. The medicine had gone straight to my throat and heart chakras. When I was six years old, I had been hit by a car and my jaw was wired shut for eight weeks. I could not speak. My voice had been physically silenced, and that silence became emotional. Though I recovered on the outside, the imprint of being unheard echoed quietly through the years.

I became articulate and expressive, building a career on my ability to communicate. I led teams, presented to executives, and coached clients with confidence. And yet, personal relationships were a different story. I avoided confrontation, suppressed discomfort, and mistook peacekeeping for peace. Each time I swallowed my truth, resentment grew in the space where authenticity should have lived.

Eventually, my body began to express what I would not. Jaw pain, teeth grinding, and TMJ surfaced as physical reminders of emotional suppression. It first appeared in my thirties during a painful chapter in my life, and again in my fifties while working for a leader whose values deeply conflicted with my own. Both times, I stayed silent for too long, and both times, I eventually walked away.

Today, I still notice when I begin to withhold my truth. The signs are subtle but familiar: the tightness in my jaw, the heaviness in my heart, the exhaustion that comes from pretending. When they appear, I pause and ask myself one question: *Am I being heard, or am I merely enduring?*

Because healing begins not when others finally listen, but when we are heard.

Reclaiming the Power of Your Voice

Your voice is not a luxury, it's a lifeline to your truth, your boundaries, and your becoming. Suppressing your voice to avoid conflict or maintain harmony often creates internal dissonance. Sovereignty begins when you choose to speak, not just when it's easy, but when it's essential. This chapter invites you to move from silence rooted in fear to expression grounded in self-respect.

Reflect

Reflection helps you notice where you've been quiet not out of peace, but out of fear. Whether it's in personal relationships, professional spaces, or within your own inner dialogue, avoiding your truth to keep others comfortable can leave lasting emotional and physical residue. Awareness is the first step toward reclaiming your voice.

- Identify where in your life you've been staying silent to avoid tension or disapproval.

- Reflect on moments where you've sacrificed your truth for the sake of keeping others comfortable.
- Pay attention to the signals your body and emotions give when you're not being heard. Is there tension, fatigue, resentment or anxiety?

Journaling Prompt: *What am I not saying and what is the cost of continuing to hold it in?*

Reframe

Reframing allows you to see that speaking your truth is not harmful, it's healing. Your voice doesn't have to be loud or confrontational to be powerful. When used with care and clarity, your words become a tool for self-honoring, healthy boundaries, and real connection.

- Speaking up isn't selfish, it's a radical act of self-respect.
- Silence that avoids conflict often breeds inner chaos.
- Your voice is sacred, not because it demands attention, but because it expresses truth.

Mantra: *My voice is not a disruption. It is a declaration of my worth.*

Reconnect

Reconnection is about building the muscle of self-expression through practice, presence, and courage. It's not about saying everything, everywhere, all at once.

It's about starting where you are, choosing safe spaces, and honoring the voice you've long been silencing. Let your words serve as a bridge between your inner knowing and the world that needs to hear it.

- **Clarify Your Needs**
  Write down what you need. Say it aloud to yourself. Then, practice expressing it clearly and calmly to others.

- **Speak Truth in Safe Spaces**
  Practice with friends, mentors, or in a journal. Let your voice strengthen in places of support before bringing it into harder conversations.

- **Speak for Your Younger Self**
  Visualize the version of you who couldn't speak up. What would she want you to say now? Say it for her and for you.

- **Evaluate the Space**
  Ask: "Is this a relationship where both voices matter?" If the answer is no, that clarity may be the truth you need to honor.

Affirmation: *I honor my voice as sacred. I speak with clarity, courage, and care because I matter.*

Final Thought: Speak from the Heart, Even When It Shakes

Your voice is not a weapon.
It is a bridge.
It spans misunderstanding and clarity.
It connects silence with self-respect.

You don't have to yell to be heard.
Nor wound another to be honest.
You only need to honor what's true.
Even when your voice trembles.

Courage is not loud.
It is steady.
It is the breath before truth.
It is choosing what matters most.

Words rooted in love become light.
Gentle truth still carries power.
Integrity, spoken consistently, echoes.
Love rewrites the story of your worth.

This is Sovereign Living.

Part Two

BUSINESS

REDEFINING SUCCESS THROUGH SERVICE, GRACE & GROWTH

Business, at its highest form, is not a hustle; it is harmony. It is where intuition meets action and purpose becomes prosperity. Sovereign success is not about domination but about alignment, a way of living where wealth and well-being coexist in balance and integrity. It is the steady movement of your internal Compass, guiding each decision toward fulfillment rather than exhaustion.

In **Influence to Affluence**, you learn that influence grows from authenticity, and affluence naturally follows purpose. **Support Others to Yield Your Success** reveals the paradox of prosperity: when you lift others, you inevitably rise. **Hustle to Grace** transforms striving into flow, reminding you that ease is not laziness; it is mastery born of trust and clarity.

Problems to Solutions reframes obstacles as sacred invitations to evolve. **Failure to Growth** redefines what it means to win, showing that every misstep is a lesson in disguise. **Technology to Connectivity** invites you to use modern tools with ancient wisdom, building not just efficient systems but meaningful relationships.

Endings to Beginnings explores the transformative power hidden within life's closures, reminding us that endings are not punishments but sacred pivots, opportunities to release the past and realign with deeper truth. **Random Relations to Sphere of Influence** expands this awareness outward, transforming casual connections into intentional relationships built on integrity and mutual growth. **Most Important to Most Respected & Influential** deepens that lesson, helping you move beyond external metrics of success to cultivate genuine leadership, where respect is earned through consistency, character and compassion.

White Space to Closing the Gap teaches the power of pause, showing how clarity and timing can bridge the distance between vision and action, creating space for innovation, connection, and meaningful results. **Fixed Mindset to Growth Mindset** continues this evolution, reframing uncertainty as a sacred space for transformation and inviting you to embrace the unknown as the birthplace of creativity and purpose.

Business, in its Sovereign form, becomes a conscious enterprise rooted in service, integrity, and meaningful growth. It is how you learn to follow your Compass in the material world, to create, connect, and contribute with both vision and purpose. This is not the pursuit of profit alone, but the cultivation of impact, alignment, and legacy that endures over time.

INFLUENCE TO AFFLUENCE

"Every opportunity, every influence and affluence you possess could not have been for you alone, but to act as a platform to impact a generation."
~ Sunday Adelaja

Actors, athletes, musicians, entrepreneurs, and influencers all share one thing in common: powerful reach. Fans follow their every move, celebrate their wins, excuse their losses, and imitate their choices from sneakers to skincare, cars to causes. For a brand strategist, it can seem like a dream come true: a built-in audience, massive influence, effortless revenue.

But what if that influence could be used for something greater than accumulation? Because at some point, more becomes just more. More to manage, more to insure, more to lose, and ultimately, less time to live. Real success asks a different question: not "How much can I gain?" but "How deeply can I give?"

A New Definition of Affluence

True affluence is not about what you have; it is about what you give. You do not need millions to make an impact. You do not need a nonprofit or a massive following. What you need is a willingness to serve with your time, your talent, your energy, and your love.

Influence becomes affluence the moment you choose contribution over accumulation, when presence becomes purpose, and success becomes service.

My Story: Giving for Fulfillment - Mine + Theirs

While raising my children, volunteering was part of our rhythm: school fairs, sports teams, libraries, and Girl Scouts. I showed up. It felt natural and fulfilling. But one vision lingered for years. I wanted to take my children to volunteer at a soup kitchen.

We never made it happen, not for lack of care but simply because of life's constant motion. Then I moved to Malibu, and the contrast was striking. Beautiful coastline. Oceanfront estates. And visible homelessness. *How could such extreme wealth and suffering coexist in the same zip code?* The question stayed with me.

Soon after, I found a local outreach group that served weekly meals to unhoused neighbors. I signed up, thinking it would be a one-time thing, but it quickly became a ritual. We cooked in the donated kitchen at Serra Retreat and hand-delivered meals around town. Both my younger daughter, and my niece, Sydney, joined and supported with enthusiasm and heart.

That's where I met Carol Moss, founder of CART (Community Assistance Resource Team), known by many as "the homeless mother of Malibu." Carol was a force! She was smart, grounded, and fierce in her advocacy. She reminded me of what one person with conviction and compassion can do. Each week, we prepared lunches and dinners and served seconds with a smile. It never felt like enough, but the gratitude in their eyes said otherwise. Over time, I realized what we were really offering wasn't just food. It was acknowledgment, connection, and dignity, as well as the nourishment of being seen and cared for.

How to Claim (or Reclaim) Your Quiet Power

True power isn't always loud, visible, or tied to status. Often, it resides in the quiet spaces, in presence, in compassion, and in choosing to respond rather than react. Reclaiming your quiet power means recognizing the subtle but significant influence you already carry and choosing to wield it with clarity, purpose, and love. You don't need permission to lead; you simply need to remember that your life already speaks.

Reflect

To reflect is to become aware of where your influence already lives which often is in places you've overlooked or undervalued. Notice who listens when you speak, who turns to you in need, and what parts of the world keep pulling at your heart. You may find that leadership isn't something to be earned, but something to be remembered.

- Identify areas of your life where your presence already carries weight, family, profession, community.
- Notice what others naturally seek from you: perspective, peace, clarity, organization.
- Pay attention to recurring causes or needs that stir you emotionally. These are clues to your deeper calling.

Journaling Prompt: *Where do I already hold unacknowledged influence, and how could acknowledging it shift how I show up in the world?*

Reframe

Reframing invites you to shift the lens through which you view power, value, and service. Influence isn't a title or a platform, it's a way of being. When you begin to see your awareness, integrity, and presence as forms of wealth, your contribution becomes both grounded and expansive.

- Influence is not reserved for the famous or loud. Your intentional presence has impact.
- Your affluence lies in your awareness and your ability to show up with wisdom, not just resources.
- You don't need to fix everything. Begin with one sincere action that aligns with who you are.

Empowering Question: *What if my presence is already enough to shift the energy in a room?*

Reconnect

To reconnect is to bring your gifts back into service, not through striving, but through alignment. What have you dismissed or forgotten about yourself that might be deeply needed by others? When you offer what's natural to you, service becomes sustainable, and purpose becomes real.

- Reclaim an overlooked strength, talent, or relationship and ask how it could uplift someone else.
- Offer your energy, through time, support, or wisdom in spaces aligned with your core values.
- Engage in meaningful collaboration. Let your influence multiply through shared vision and connection.

Affirmation: *I honor the power I carry, and I use it with intention, grace, and love.*

Final Thought: Influence Is Your Currency, Spend It Well

Influence is your currency.
Affluence is how you spend it.
True wealth isn't measured by what you collect,
it's remembered by what you give:
Your presence. Your courage. Your care.

You weren't given your voice, your gifts,
or your position by accident.
They're not trophies, they're tools.
Tools meant to build bridges, not pedestals.

Affluence doesn't come from having more.
It comes from becoming more.
More generous. More aware. More available to others.

You don't have to change the whole world.
But you *can* change someone's world,
simply by showing up with what you already have.

That's real influence.
That's lasting legacy.
That's the path of the Sovereign.
That's true wealth.

This is Sovereign Living.

SUPPORT OTHERS TO YIELD YOUR SUCCESS

"Success comes in direct proportion to the number of people you help."

~ Will Craig

True success is never a solo pursuit, it's a symphony of shared growth. Every time you lift another, you elevate yourself. The world often glorifies independence, but the real mark of Sovereignty lies in interdependence: the courage to celebrate others' light without dimming your own. When you help someone rise, you expand the field of possibility for everyone, including yourself.

Supporting others is not self-sacrifice; it's self-mastery. It's understanding that generosity doesn't diminish your worth, it multiplies it. When you freely share your wisdom, offer mentorship, or celebrate another's success, you affirm abundance over scarcity. The heart that cheers for others creates an ecosystem of reciprocity, where collaboration replaces competition and unity becomes the new form of power.

To yield your success through support is to lead from wholeness. It's choosing to see life not as a race, but as a relay, where every handoff strengthens the legacy. Your influence grows in direct proportion to the number of people you help rise. The more you nurture, the more you're nourished. This is the quiet truth of sustainable success, when your win becomes *our* win, and your purpose becomes service in motion.

My Story: Service to Success

In real estate, I made a choice early on that others didn't understand: I chose to serve the university students.

Colleagues asked, "Why waste your time on kids renting small places?" But I didn't see it that way. I saw an opportunity, not just for business, but for connection.

Helping students find safe, affordable housing wasn't glamorous, but it was meaningful. I answered their calls. I walked them through lease terms. I explained credit, co-signers, and utilities. I met with their parents and treated them like future homeowners.

And guess what? That investment paid off. Today, nearly 90% of my business, from luxury home sales to referrals, grew organically from that original decision to support a community few prioritized.

Later, I partnered with a younger agent, Izzy. She brought digital fluency and social savvy. I brought a decade of local knowledge and experience. We supported each other. Our trust and collaboration doubled our listings, expanded our clientele, and created a multi-generational brand that neither of us could have built alone.

That's the power of service. That's the secret to sustainable success.

Success becomes more meaningful, and sustainable, when it's shared. Supporting others isn't a distraction from your growth; it's often the very path that accelerates it. When we recognize the power of mutual uplift, we move from scarcity to abundance, from competition to connection. Yielding space for others to rise is not a loss of position, it is an act of Sovereignty.

Reflect

Reflection allows you to see the lineage of support behind your own journey and recognize the opportunities to extend that same grace forward. Consider who helped you when you were uncertain, starting out, or in need of encouragement. Also, notice where you may feel triggered by others' success, not to judge, but to learn what part of you is ready to be expanded or healed.

- Remember the people who offered you encouragement, resources, or belief when you needed it most.
- Look around: who is quietly reaching out for connection, guidance, or visibility right now?
- Identify moments when someone else's success stirred discomfort in you. What did it mirror about your own desires or doubts?

Journaling Prompt: *What did someone else's support unlock in me and how can I now become that for someone else?*

Reframe

Reframing helps you see that another's light doesn't cast a shadow on yours, it actually illuminates what's possible. Supporting others doesn't require authority or a title; it simply asks for presence, willingness, and humility. When you share your insight, experience, or belief in someone else, you step into a larger version of your own leadership.

- Someone else's growth is not your competition; it's your invitation to rise together.

- Mentorship doesn't require perfection, only presence and sincerity.
- Supporting others builds trust, community, and opportunities that no solitary path can offer.

Empowering Question: *How might supporting someone else's path strengthen my own?*

Reconnect

Reconnection is about turning your awareness into action, not as a performance, but as an offering. Think of someone who could benefit from your insight or presence and extend it with no expectation of return. When you invest in others from a place of purpose, you create a deeper sense of meaning in your own journey.

- Choose one person who is new, unseen, or facing challenges. Reach out, listen, and simply be available.
- Offer a small, consistent act of mentorship, even a short monthly check-in can create lasting impact.
- Celebrate someone else's strengths. Reflect their potential back to them with authenticity and encouragement.

Affirmation: *I rise by lifting others, and in their success, I expand my own capacity for impact and joy.*

Final Thought: Support is a Seed

Support is a seed, small, but sacred.
When planted with sincerity, it grows roots of trust.
It blooms into impact, integrity, and shared success.

Give without agenda.
Guide without control.
Grow without comparison.

What you nurture in others
will one day return to you,
multiplied in ways you never imagined.
Because generosity is not a transaction, it's a legacy.

Every act of genuine support becomes
a thread in the fabric of collective rising.
When one thrives, all are lifted.
When one shines, the light expands.

The lives you help elevate
will always elevate yours in return.

This is Sovereign Living.

HUSTLE TO GRACE

*"Dolce far niente —
the sweetness of doing nothing."*
~ *Elizabeth Gilbert, an expression
popularized in the book and movie Eat Pray Love*

We live in an age that glorifies motion, where productivity is mistaken for purpose and rest is viewed as weakness. The world tells us to hustle harder, climb faster, and do more to prove our worth. Yet beneath the constant striving lies exhaustion, disconnection, and a quiet longing for peace. What if fulfillment isn't found in acceleration, but in alignment? What if the sweetness of life, *dolce far niente*, the art of doing nothing, is not idleness, but intimacy with the present moment?

For many, hustle becomes a hiding place, a way to outrun discomfort, silence grief, or mask uncertainty. Busyness is praised, but often it's a distraction from what truly matters. When our value becomes tethered to achievement, we forget that we are already enough. Grace invites us to pause, to trust that rest is not the absence of progress, but the space where wisdom gathers and creation begins anew.

To move from hustle to grace is to reclaim balance as a spiritual practice. It's remembering that your pace does not determine your purpose. In slowing down, you return to rhythm, to breath, to beauty, and to being. The shift isn't about doing less, but about doing what aligns with your highest energy. Grace is not something you earn; it's something you allow. When you live from that place, life no longer becomes a race, it becomes a flow.

My Story: Hustle to Unhustle

I was raised by an Italian immigrant father who believed in grit. His favorite saying still echoes in my mind: "If you want something done, do it yourself." By twelve, I had a paper route. By fifteen, a retail job. I worked full time while attending university. By adulthood, I was a goal-setter, a go-getter, always striving and always achieving. The hustle became my heartbeat.

But eventually, that relentless drive caught up with me. I burned out. I lost momentum, money, and a bit of faith in myself. For the first time, I had to ask for help and it humbled me. Yet in that humility, something shifted. I began to rebuild, not through force, but through flow.

I started tracking my spending, building sustainable income, and releasing unnecessary hours. I replaced overworking with spending more time with family, practicing yoga, writing, and rest. Slowly, life began to respond differently. The more I surrendered, the more I received; the right clients, the right opportunities, and the right rhythm.

I stopped hustling and started aligning. What once felt like a grind began to feel like grace. I learned that productivity without peace is just performance and that true success is not built on exhaustion, but on ease.

How to Shift Hustle and Grit to Presence

The world often teaches us that success must be earned through relentless hustle, but true Sovereignty comes when we choose grace over grind. Shifting from constant doing to intentional being is not a sign of weakness; it's a radical return to your innate wisdom. When your worth is no longer tied to your productivity, you create space for peace, power, and purpose to emerge.

Reflect

To reflect is to examine where your beliefs about worth and success were formed and how they may still be driving you today. Ask yourself where you learned that being busy equals being valuable, and what discomfort you may be avoiding through constant motion. Becoming aware of these patterns allows you to gently disrupt them.

- Recall when you first began to equate hustle or overworking with achievement or approval.
- Notice how often your sense of self-worth is linked to your output or productivity.
- Explore what feelings or truths you may be avoiding by staying constantly "busy."

Journaling Prompt: *What am I trying to prove by staying busy and who am I trying to prove it to?*

Reframe

Reframing invites you to see rest not as an indulgence, but as an essential act of power and clarity. Grace is not passive, it is a steady, intentional rhythm that aligns you with your truest self. When you allow stillness, you create space for wisdom to rise and for your actions to be guided from a place of alignment rather than exhaustion.

- Stillness is not the opposite of success, it is the soil

from which sustainable success grows.

- Slowing down allows you to access deeper clarity and more meaningful decisions.

- True productivity isn't about doing more, but about doing what matters, with peace.

Mantra: *I do not hustle to prove my worth. I move with grace because I know it.*

Reconnect

Reconnection asks you to integrate what you've remembered into how you live. You shift from pushing harder to listening deeper to your body, your spirit, and your needs. Begin to build small sacred pauses into your daily rhythm, and let your version of success be defined by alignment, not exhaustion.

- Carve out intentional moments of stillness each day, even ten minutes can soften your pace and sharpen your presence.

- Start your day with practices that center you before external demands e.g. breathwork, yoga, silence, gratitude.

- Redefine your relationship with success and money: let them serve your well-being, not control it.

Affirmation: *I am worthy of rest, aligned with peace, and guided by grace.*

Final Thought: Stop Chasing and Let it Be

You don't have to outrun your life.
You already belong within it.
Success is not a finish line.
It is a feeling, a rhythm.

It is a return to yourself.
What you seek isn't in the hustle.
It lives in postponed quiet moments.
Grace whispers where grind once shouted.

Stillness reveals what striving hides.
When chasing stops, clarity arrives.
When proving ends, peace enters.
When performing fades, purpose rises.

Let your life soften.
Let your nervous system settle.
Measure worth by presence, not productivity.
What's meant for you finds its way home.

This is Sovereign Living.

PROBLEMS TO SOLUTIONS

"Solutions are connected to the problems, and you are connected to the solutions."

~ Hiral Nagda

Every problem contains its own wisdom, a coded invitation to clarity. Yet, when faced with difficulty, our instinct is often to look everywhere but within. We seek validation, collect advice, and gather perspectives until we drown in opinions. But true resolution begins not with reaction, but reflection. The moment we stop scrambling for answers and start listening inward, we reconnect with the intelligence that lives beneath the noise, the part of us that already knows the way.

Problems are not punishments; they're portals. Each one reveals where energy is misaligned or where truth is waiting to be seen. When we pause long enough to trace a challenge to its root, not just the surface symptoms, solutions begin to surface naturally. Clarity doesn't shout; it whispers. It emerges in stillness, in presence, and in the quiet confidence that we are not separate from the solution, but inseparable from its unfolding.

To move from problems to solutions is to shift from panic to power. It's remembering that uncertainty is not your enemy, it's an initiation into deeper awareness. Every obstacle becomes an opportunity to refine your focus, strengthen your intuition, and lead from your inner Compass. When you trust your own wisdom, you stop chasing answers and start embodying them. This is the essence of Sovereign problem-solving: grace under pressure, clarity through calm, and wisdom born from within.

My Story: Learning to Lead from Within

Early in my corporate marketing career, I hit a wall. I was managing a product launch under a demanding timeline with almost no budget. The pressure was relentless. I sought everyone's input; peers, senior staff, even my partner at the time. The more advice I received, the more tangled I became.

That's when a mentor pulled me aside and said something I'll never forget: "Every solution you need already exists within you; you simply need to understand the origin of the problem."

That moment shifted everything. Instead of reacting, I paused. I defined the core issue. I traced its cause. I imagined the cost of inaction. From that grounded place, the solution emerged and it worked. Since then, I've trained myself to slow down, observe, and listen inward before reaching outward.

One memorable example came while consulting for a wellness retreat center in Costa Rica. Bookings were not increasing at the expected rate, and we had zero marketing budget. Instead of panicking, I looked within the data for clues. Surveys revealed that most guests came via word-of-mouth and they were overwhelmingly women aged 45–65 from Southern California, seeking rest, emotional healing, and a renewed sense of purpose.

With that insight, we pivoted quickly:

- We provided enhanced spa offerings that fully relaxed mind, body, and spirit.
- Launched a social-proof campaign using real guest stories to illuminate the problem to transformation.

- Created new healing and empowerment workshops through a weekly speaker series to address real struggles with real solutions.

It worked. Not because we spent more, but because we listened deeper. Every challenge holds a quiet answer. You just have to be still enough to hear it.

How to Turn Pressure into Possibility

Problems are not interruptions to your path, they are invitations to deepen your clarity, expand your thinking, and return to trust. When you stop reacting and start listening, solutions often rise from within. This chapter guides you to move from scattered urgency to steady insight, transforming challenges into gateways for growth.

Reflect

Reflection is about noticing your automatic reactions and beginning to question them. When a challenge shows up, do you overthink, seek external validation, or avoid it altogether? Getting honest about your patterns allows you to access the wisdom beneath them, the inner voice that often gets drowned out in noise.

- Identify your typical response to stress or challenge. Do you freeze, fixate, or flee?
- Ask yourself how much you rely on outside input instead of trusting your internal Compass.
- Remember a time when a clear solution came only after you slowed down or tuned in.

Journaling Prompt: *What are my go-to patterns when I face a problem and what might they be protecting me from?*

Reframe

Reframing shifts the narrative from punishment to purpose. Problems don't appear to derail you, they appear to redirect you. The path to resolution is rarely about having all the answers right away, but about being present enough to ask the right questions and listen for what's true.

- See problems not as blocks, but as prompts for clarity, growth, or realignment.
- Focus on identifying the root issue rather than rushing to fix symptoms.
- Trust that presence often delivers more insight than excessive analysis.

Insight Practice: *The solution lives in the space between urgency and awareness.*

Reconnect

Reconnection is the bridge between insight and action. When a challenge arises, create space to respond with intention rather than react from fear. A simple framework can turn overwhelm into traction and presence into progress.

- **Identify the Problem**
  Write it out clearly. What's happening, and how is it impacting you or others?

- **Understand the Implications**
Ask: "What happens if nothing changes? Let the discomfort sharpen your clarity."

- **Offer 1–2 Solutions**
Start small. Look to past wins, intuition, or even a quiet pause for guidance.

Bonus Application: In group settings or leadership conversations, model solution-based thinking. Try: "Here's the situation. Here's my perspective. Here's a proposed path forward." This approach replaces pressure with partnership.

Affirmation: *I meet challenges with clarity, trust, and the wisdom to find a way forward.*

Final Thought: Sovereignty Through Solution

You were never meant to outsource your power.
You were never meant to fear life's problems.
You were meant to meet them,
with presence, patience, and clarity.

Every challenge carries a whisper of wisdom.
Every obstacle conceals a hidden door.
Solutions are not found, they are revealed,
when you return to stillness and listen within.

You are not broken.
You are being refined.
The answers you seek are already forming,
waiting for your calm, your courage, your trust.

When you meet life as a partner, not a puzzle,
you rise as the Compass itself,
steady, Sovereign, and sure of direction.

This is Sovereign Living.

FAILURE TO GROWTH

*"If you never failed,
you never tried anything new."*
~ Albert Einstein

Failure is not a verdict, it's a revelation. In a culture that worships success and hides struggle, we often forget that every meaningful triumph is built on moments of falling and rising again. Failure strips away illusion, humbles the ego, and invites us back to authenticity. It asks: "Who are you when things don't go your way? What remains when the titles, applause, and plans fall away?" When we stop fearing failure, we begin learning from it and that shift transforms shame into strength.

Every failure carries a lesson wrapped in disguise. It's not punishment; it's precision. Life uses these moments to refine your discernment, redirect your energy, and strengthen your inner foundation. The collapse, the loss, the disappointment each one contains an encoded truth about what no longer fits and what's waiting to emerge. Seen through the lens of curiosity rather than criticism, failure becomes sacred feedback. It doesn't define you, it develops you.

To move from failure to growth is to embrace the art of beginning again. It's the courage to stand in your own debris and still declare, I am becoming. This is the alchemy of evolution; the quiet, Sovereign knowing that falling is not the opposite of flying, but part of learning how to soar. Growth doesn't erase the fall; it honors it. Because every time you rise, you rise wiser, freer, and more aligned with your truth.

My Story: Failure Reveals What Truly Matters

I've failed more than once. I've failed in relationships, in business, and in finances. I've made choices that felt right in the moment, only to watch them unravel and reveal lessons I wasn't ready to see. There were seasons when I wore every hat, spun every plate, and still couldn't hold it all together. I mistook busyness for purpose and achievement for worth.

When the collapse came, it was both painful and clarifying. It forced me to pause and strip down to truth. I began asking myself better questions: *Who actually deserves my time, energy, and love? What relationships bring energy back into my life? Where am I over giving and under-receiving?*

I ran what I now call my 80/20 audit: eighty percent of my peace, prosperity, and fulfillment were coming from just twenty percent of my effort and relationships. The rest was noise and distraction dressed as duty. That realization changed everything. I learned that failure doesn't just expose weakness; it reveals alignment. It shows you what matters most, what's worth keeping, what needs releasing, and what's been quietly waiting for you to begin again. Failure didn't break me. It built the wiser, truer version of me: the one who no longer fears falling because she knows she'll always rise.

As a mother, one of the greatest gifts I could give my children was to let them see me fail, not just stumble, but rise again with grace, humility, and Sovereignty. Just as importantly, I allow them to fail too, not from neglect, but from love. I support; I do not shield. Because every failure carries the seed of self-discovery if we're brave enough to let it grow.

How to Transform Setbacks into Self-Mastery

Failure is not the opposite of growth, it's often the gateway to it. What feels like a collapse is usually a call to deeper alignment, self-honesty, and courage. When you stop resisting failure and start listening to what it reveals, you unlock the kind of wisdom that can't be learned through winning alone. This chapter invites you to reimagine failure as a catalyst for your next evolution.

Reflect

Reflection invites you to look back not to regret, but to understand. When you recall a moment of failure, what internal narrative took over? Whose voices did you believe, and how did it shape what you thought was possible for you afterward? Examining your response to failure reveals where you may still be holding shame or where new strength is ready to emerge.

- Recall a time you felt you had failed. What story did you begin to tell yourself about who you are?
- Consider whether growth came from that moment, even if it arrived later or in disguise.
- Reflect on who supported you and who didn't. What did their responses teach you about trust, value, or expectations?

Journaling Prompt: *What did I make that failure mean about me and what's a more truthful, empowering story I can tell now?*

Reframe

Reframing transforms failure from a dead end into a directional signal. Failure doesn't mean you are unworthy; it often means you were out of alignment with your values, timing, or truth. Seen clearly, failure becomes feedback and with it, the choice to move forward with more clarity, courage, and authenticity.

- Failure reflects where something wasn't working, not where you are broken.

- Use the insight from failure to realign with your deeper self, not to retreat in shame.

- Recognize failure as motion, not stagnation. It means you were trying, risking, learning.

Mantra: *I do not fear failure. I welcome what it teaches me and who it helps me become.*

Reconnect

Reconnection turns experience into embodied wisdom. When you own the lessons from your missteps and share them from a place of wholeness, you turn pain into purpose. This process isn't about fixing the past, it's about using it as fertile ground for growth, connection, and service.

- **Own the Lesson**
  Be honest and specific. Name the misstep without judgment. "I ignored my intuition." "I rushed." "I avoided the truth."

- **Rewrite the Story**
  Replace self-blame with strategy. Speak to yourself like a mentor would. "Now I know." "This made me wiser." "I am still worthy."

- **Share It**
  Let your vulnerability serve others; whether it's a friend, a mentee, or your own child. Speak your experience with empathy, not ego.

Affirmation: *My past does not define me. I grow from every experience, and I lead with the wisdom I've earned.*

Final Thought: Redefine Failure

The people we admire most, the icons, the visionaries, the ones who changed the world, failed more times than they succeeded.

But they didn't stop.
They transformed.
They turned rejection into redirection,
and disappointment into design.

Every fall refined their focus.
Every ending revealed a beginning.
Every "no" shaped the strength to find a better "yes."

Let your setbacks sculpt your wisdom,
not your worth.
Let them temper your spirit,
not tarnish your belief.

Failure isn't the opposite of success,
it's the pathway that builds it.
Walk it boldly.

This is Sovereign Living.

TECHNOLOGY TO CONNECTIVITY

"If we continue to develop our technology without wisdom or prudence, our servant may prove to be our executioner."
~ *General Omar Bradley*

We live in a time when technology is both our greatest tool and our greatest distraction. According to Reviews.org, Americans check our phones an average of 205 times a day, yet most of us can't remember what we saw that truly mattered. Is it really making us more productive? Or simply busier, more fragmented, more disconnected from ourselves?

According to the U.S. Bureau of Labor Statistics; since 2005, U.S. labor productivity has grown by less than 2% annually, despite the explosion of smartphones, apps, and "always-on" connectivity. Meanwhile, rates of anxiety, burnout, and loneliness have soared, proving that efficiency doesn't always equal enrichment.

The truth is, technology is neutral. It is neither savior nor villain. It becomes sacred only when used with intention, serving as a bridge to presence, purpose, and genuine human connection, rather than a barrier that separates us from them.

My Story: Intentional Systems, Aligned Living

As someone who transitioned from the corporate world into real estate entrepreneurship, and now evolving into service-led leadership, technology has always been a part of my work but never my identity.

Early on, I was a PC person. Then I fell in love with my iPhone. Eventually, I migrated to Mac; not because I'm a tech person, but because I finally saw how certain tools simplified my life and helped me move through each day with more ease and flow.

What helped most wasn't the "latest" app; it was being intentional. I made peace with the fact that I didn't need to be an expert in everything, but I did need to create a system that matched my values, my rhythm, and my energy, not someone else's version of success.

Whether it was syncing calendars across devices, organizing passwords, or curating apps that actually helped me focus, I began to see how technology could support my Sovereignty rather than steal it. I still review and refine those tools often. When life gets noisy or chaotic, digital clutter only adds to it. Clearing it, even just deleting old apps or organizing files, brings peace and clarity back.

Because technology isn't just about how we communicate with others. It's about how we relate to ourselves and how we preserve the space between noise and knowing so that connection remains intentional, not automatic.

Turning Tech into a Tool for Presence

Technology can either deepen your connection to what matters or scatter your focus and deplete your energy. It's not the device that determines your experience, but the intention behind how you use it. Sovereignty with technology means reclaiming your time, clarity, and relationships by using tools to support your life, not steal from it.

Reflect

To reflect is to become aware of how technology currently shapes your energy, attention, and presence. It's not about guilt or judgment, but about clarity: Where are your devices helping you connect and where are they subtly creating disconnection? When you notice your patterns honestly, you can begin to shift them.

- Ask yourself whether your devices are supporting your values or simply consuming your time.
- Notice when you feel most mentally scattered or emotionally drained. What role does tech play in those moments?
- Identify your most-used apps or platforms. Are they tools for growth or just reflexive distractions?

Journaling Prompt: *How is my current use of technology reflecting, or distorting, the life I want to live?*

Reframe

Reframing your relationship with technology means shifting from unconscious consumption to intentional use. Tech isn't inherently harmful, but distraction is. When you organize your digital life with clarity, you create space for presence, purpose, and peace. Used wisely, technology becomes an amplifier of connection, not a substitute for it.

- Technology is not the enemy, misuse is. What you consume shapes how you feel.
- Your attention is your most valuable resource. Every click, scroll, and notification is a decision.

- Systems and automations don't limit freedom, they create it by protecting your mental bandwidth.

Empowering Question: *Am I using technology to connect more deeply or to escape what I don't want to feel?*

Reconnect

Reconnection invites you to realign your digital habits with your core values. Through simple but powerful shifts, you can turn your devices into allies that support clarity, creativity, and meaningful engagement. It's not about perfection, it's about presence.

- **Calendar with Clarity**
  Use your digital calendar as sacred space. Color-code by category. Set reminders for what truly matters. Structure can liberate.

- **Simplify & Streamline**
  Audit your apps. Remove the excess. Organize by use. A clean digital space reflects a clear mind.

- **Automate & Protect**
  Automate recurring tasks like bill payments or appointment scheduling. Use password managers. Create simple systems to safeguard your time and energy.

- **Create Tech-Free Time Zones**
  Designate device-free moments, especially mornings and evenings. Use built-in tools to manage screen time. Protect your peace proactively.

- **Convert Distraction into Development**
  Replace mindless scrolling with intentional learning or reflection. Ten minutes a day adds up and reclaims your focus.

Affirmation: *I use technology with intention. It serves my life, it does not run it.*

Final Thought: Be the User, Not the Used

Technology should amplify your presence,
not diminish it.

When you lead your tools,
instead of letting them lead you,
you move from reaction to creation.

Use tech to create space,
not clutter.
Connection,
not comparison.

Let every click be conscious,
every notification a choice,
every moment online an extension of your purpose.

Your time is sacred.
Your energy is currency.
Your attention is power.

Spend them where it matters.
Live as the Sovereign, not the scrolled.

This is Sovereign Living.

ENDINGS TO BEGINNINGS

*"When one door closes,
another one opens."*
~ Alexander Graham Bell

Every ending holds a quiet promise of renewal. When a chapter closes, it can feel painful, uncertain, or even unfair. Yet, behind every closed door is a sacred invitation to begin again. Endings are not punishments; they are pivots. They ask us to loosen our grip on what was and turn toward what is waiting. The most courageous act is not to force something to remain but to trust that release is the first step toward redirection.

To move forward, you must let go with grace. When you no longer linger at the threshold of what has passed, you create space for new alignment to unfold. Endings are teachers in disguise, reminding us that every pause holds potential and every loss contains the seed of a beginning. They are not the conclusion of your story but the refinement of your Compass, guiding you back to truth.

Each closing chapter clears the clutter of what no longer fits your evolution. When you release what has run its course, you make room for something far more extraordinary than you could have imagined. Life rewards your willingness to surrender with unexpected beauty: new opportunities, deeper connections, and a stronger, wiser version of yourself. Endings are not the opposite of beginnings; they are the passageway between who you were and who you are becoming.

My Story: Gracefully Releasing, Powerfully Receiving

There was a season when personal and professional endings collided like two waves crashing at once. After my marital separation I cautiously began dating a client from a major consumer brand I supported. We were intentional on how and where we interacted to ensure our personal and professional experiences remained separate. It felt private, contained, and safely tucked away. Until it wasn't.

Client budget cuts hit. The agency contract we held was dissolved. My role disappeared. I lost my job and my relationship at the same time. Was it personal? Maybe. But what mattered more was how I chose to respond.

This news came the same day I was set to travel to Orlando, FL with my youngest daughter and her cheer team for a Nationals competition. I said nothing to anyone about the loss of a contract or my job. I packed my bags and packed my fear away. I immersed myself in her joy, her teammates' laughter, and the simple magic of being present. That weekend changed everything.

When I returned to the agency on Monday, I showed up with grace. I finished every project, transitioned accounts with professionalism, and walked out not bitter but clear, with my dignity intact. Privately, I reignited my professional network, refreshed my résumé, and aligned my energy to receive new possibilities. Within two weeks, I landed a consulting role with NIVEA, a global skincare brand. This was a dream opportunity and only twenty minutes from home. Even more incredible, my first assignment involved a global sponsorship with none other than Rihanna and her iconic *LOUD* Tour, a full-circle moment with one of my all-time favorite artist.

But what I gained most was unexpected: Kimberly, a soul-sister and lifelong friend born of that new chapter. A woman who lives in her truth and consistently supports and serves other women personally and professionally.

Endings are never random. When you release with intention, life responds with alignment. Each closing chapter refines your direction, guiding you closer to your truth, your freedom, and your next beginning.

Letting Go to Let Life In

Endings often feel like loss, but they are also the soil from which beginnings grow. When something concludes, whether by choice or circumstance, we are given the chance to reflect, realign, and reimagine. Instead of resisting closure, we can honor it, clear space, and invite in what's next. The end of one chapter doesn't mean the story is over; it means you're being called to write the next one with deeper clarity and truth.

Reflect

Reflection helps you explore your emotional response to endings, both past and present. It's not about rushing to make meaning, but about acknowledging what was real and recognizing what's now complete. Often, endings bring not just grief but also unexpected gifts such as clarity, redirection, and release.

- Recall a significant ending in your life. What emotions surfaced? Were they grief, fear, relief, guilt?
- What unfolded in the aftermath? Did you discover new strength, direction, or insight?
- Consider who stayed and who left. Whose presence felt like true support, and who no longer needs a seat at your table?

Journaling Prompt: *What am I still holding onto that has already ended and what would it feel like to finally let it go?*

Reframe

Reframing endings allows you to see them not as failures, but as transitions. What ends is often clearing space for something more aligned, more honest, or more necessary. You may not always get closure in the form you expect, but you can choose to close the chapter with intention and self-trust.

- Endings are not rejection, they are redirection toward greater alignment.
- Closure may come without answers. The wisdom is in trusting what's unfolding, even if you can't yet explain it.
- You are not defined by what ended. You are shaped by what you learned, and how you choose to begin again.

Mantra: *I trust that what has ended is making space for what is meant for me.*

Reconnect

Reconnection is how you bring ritual, presence, and intention into the transition. Letting go isn't passive, it's an act of Sovereignty. When you honor what was, clear what no longer belongs, and open yourself to possibility, you shift from being stuck in the past to being rooted in the present and open to the future.

- **Honor the Ending**
  Write a letter to the chapter that's closing. Name your feelings honestly. Burn it, bury it, or keep it. Just let it be seen.

- **Clean the Space**
  Make a physical or digital shift. Clear your desk, delete old messages, remove symbols of what no longer fits.

- **Open Your Energy**
  Begin your mornings with rituals of invitation. Light a candle. Meditate. Speak your readiness: "I am open to what is next."

- **Choose Presence**
  Stay grounded during uncertainty. Let stillness replace panic. Trust that the unfolding is working *for* you.

Affirmation: *I release what has ended. I honor what was. I welcome what is becoming.*

Final Thought: Let Go With Grace, Receive With Faith

Every ending holds a hidden gift.
It may not appear right away.
It may not look like what you imagined.
But it is always, always there.

Bless what's done.
Thank it for what it taught.
Honor what it revealed.
Then loosen your grip.

Let the old chapter close —
not in resistance, but in reverence.
Let faith become the bridge
between what was and what will be.

Walk forward with open hands,
with heart unarmored,
ready to receive what's already reaching for you.

Something beautiful is on its way.

This is Sovereign Living.

RANDOM RELATIONS TO A REFINED SPHERE OF INFLUENCE

"You are the average of the five people you spend the most time with."

~ *Dan Peña*

Take a moment and look around your life. Who are the five people you interact with most? Family, friends, colleagues, or clients anyone consistently receiving your time, energy, and attention. These connections are not random; they are the architects of your evolution. The company you keep influences your thoughts, your habits, your energy, and ultimately, your destiny.

Your closest relationships should:

- Love you as you are, without condition.
- Celebrate your wins without envy.
- Offer honest feedback with kindness.
- Inspire your growth through example.
- Uplift your spirit when you forget your own light.

Refining your sphere of influence is not about elitism, it is about energetic alignment. As you evolve, the vibration of your relationships must evolve too. The people you allow closest to you should expand your vision, not shrink it. Some connections are seasonal, arriving to teach you lessons or mirror your growth edges. Others are lifelong allies, soul companions who walk beside you in purpose, truth, and mutual respect.

Honoring both requires discernment. When you begin to curate your circle with intention, you shift from seeking approval to embodying authenticity. You stop chasing belonging and begin attracting resonance. The result is not isolation; it is elevation. You rise, surrounded by those who reflect your highest self back to you.

My Story: Curating Connection with Conscious Care

For me, my treasured "five" are the pillars of my emotional and energetic ecosystem. Even when we aren't in daily contact, they occupy the most meaningful space in my heart and mind. Each one reflects a different dimension of my growth: the grounded friend who listens without judgment, the visionary who inspires me to dream bigger, the truth-teller who reminds me to stay accountable, the nurturer who offers warmth without words, and the spiritual ally who prays for me even when I forget to pray for myself. They are grounded, forward-focused, and rooted in compassion.

Around that inner circle are others whose strength anchors family, those who remind me that love continues in new forms, and those who show up with authenticity and warmth, woven together by mutual trust and respect. Each relationship carries its own frequency, some deeply personal, others professional, yet all aligned in reciprocity and integrity. Beyond the seen, there is the unseen: God, guardian angels, saints, and family members who've crossed over. They form an invisible network of grace that guides and protects me daily, reminding me that I am never truly alone.

I didn't always curate this circle so consciously. For years, I allowed proximity, obligation, and old narratives to decide who had access to my energy. I mistook familiarity for loyalty and equated longevity with alignment. But through grief, healing, and spiritual awakening, I learned that love without boundaries drains rather than nourishes. Now, I choose presence over performance, resonance over responsibility, and peace over people-pleasing. The lesson is clear and sacred:

- Your circle is your sanctuary.
- Your energy is your currency.
- Your influence is your legacy.

Curating a Circle That Elevates You

The people you surround yourself with shape more than your time; they influence your mindset, energy, and evolution. Refining your sphere of influence doesn't mean rejecting others; it means consciously choosing who aligns with your current values and future vision. When you honor your growth, you give others permission to honor theirs and you create space for more purposeful, uplifting connection.

Reflect

To reflect is to examine who currently holds proximity to your energy and why. The people you spend time with emotionally, physically, and mentally leave a lasting imprint. By assessing how they affect your well-being, clarity, and forward momentum, you begin to take responsibility for the energy you keep around you.

- List the five people you interact with most, whether through time, thought, or conversation.
- After spending time with each, do you feel uplifted and clear or drained and doubtful?
- Are they anchored in their own growth, or are they repeating cycles you've already outgrown?

Journaling Prompt: *What kind of influence am I allowing into my life and is it reflecting who I am becoming?*

Reframe

Reframing your relationships begins with releasing guilt and reclaiming choice. Every connection doesn't need to be permanent and growth sometimes means changing proximity, not abandoning care. You don't need dramatic exits or perfect explanations. All you need is clarity about where you're going and who genuinely supports that path.

- Relationships are not life sentences, they are lived agreements that evolve as you do.
- Choosing alignment over comfort is not rejection; it's respect for your becoming.
- Guilt is not a Compass. Ask instead: "What am I choosing by staying and what might I gain by stepping back?"

Empowering Question: *What version of myself do I protect or neglect by who I keep closest?*

Reconnect

Reconnection means taking aligned, intentional steps to create a circle that energizes your purpose and reflects your growth. Your sphere should inspire, support, and stretch you. Refining your relationships doesn't mean closing your heart, it means stewarding your energy with wisdom and love.

- **Conduct a Weekly Energy Audit**
  List people, places, or tasks you've engaged with. Create two columns: Energized and Exhausted. Notice patterns.

- **Protect Your Energy Gently**
  Begin with healthy boundaries. Distance doesn't require drama. Try: "I'm entering a more intentional season and pulling my energy inward for clarity and peace."

- **Curate a Circle That Reflects Your Growth**
  Spend more time with those who challenge and nourish you. Intentionally deepen bonds with those who reflect your values.

- **Expand Through Inspiration**
  Include authors, mentors, podcasters, or thought leaders in your "inner five." Influence is not limited to proximity.

- **Visualize Your Inner Circle**
  Picture a table. Who is seated there? Who uplifts you just by presence? Who may need to gently step away so you can grow?

Affirmation: *I surround myself with people who reflect my values, honor my growth, and amplify my light.*

Final Thought: Choose Your Influence

Your energy is your currency.
Protect it like the sacred resource it is.

Surround yourself with those who
challenge you kindly,
who celebrate you genuinely,
who inspire you consistently.

Let your circle reflect your highest self,
not your history, but your horizon.
Choose people who water your roots
and cheer your blooming.

Be around those who speak possibility,
not limitation.
Presence, not pretense.
Depth, not drama.

Because your life is extraordinary
and it deserves to be mirrored
by the souls who walk beside you.

This is Sovereign Living.

MOST IMPORTANT TO MOST RESPECTED & INFLUENTIAL

"Biology deals the cards, but social conditions dictate how the game is played."
~Ted Gioia

There is a subtle but powerful difference between being important and being influential. Importance seeks validation; influence builds value. The desire to be important often stems from ego, a need to be seen, heard, or acknowledged. But respect and influence are born of integrity, consistency, and the quiet confidence that doesn't demand attention but naturally earns it.

This chapter explores what happens when leadership moves beyond self-promotion and into self-possession. It is the evolution from needing to prove yourself to allowing your presence, professionalism, and steadiness to speak for you. In this space, power is no longer a performance but a vibration that inspires trust, loyalty, and authentic connection.

Unlike **Insecure to Confident** in Part One, which focuses on the inner transformation of self-belief, **Most Important to Most Respected & Influential** invites you into the external expression of that inner work. It asks you to consider how your confidence moves in a room and how do others feel in your presence. True influence is not about being the loudest voice; it is about being the calmest anchor. It is not about leading the room; it is about elevating everyone in it.

My Story: Leading With Quiet Strength

There was a season in my career when I found myself navigating complex power dynamics among women in male-dominated industries. I noticed early on that not all tension came from overt competition. Sometimes it was more subtle, an unspoken hierarchy of beauty, confidence, style, or even proximity to influence. These quiet comparisons shaped the energy in the room far more than any formal structure of authority.

At one point, a male colleague pulled me aside after a meeting and said gently, "She likes you, Laura… just let her be the prettiest girl in the room." I was stunned. What did that even mean? Over time, I began to see that the underlying current wasn't about skill or performance. It was about perception, placement, and the quiet social competition that often lives beneath professional ambition. I learned that insecurity can sometimes disguise itself as power, and that not every rivalry needs to be met with resistance.

Instead of retreating or reacting, I chose grace. I complimented her sincerely. I affirmed her generously. And the tension dissolved. What began as quiet competition became a genuine, mutually supportive partnership. In that experience, I discovered that real strength doesn't compete for the spotlight, it steadies the light so everyone can shine. True leadership is not about asserting dominance but about creating safety, belonging, and recognition in spaces where they are often missing. Sometimes the most powerful thing you can do is let others feel seen, valued, and safe.

The Power of Presence Over Performance

True leadership doesn't need volume to be heard or

theatrics to be felt. Quiet strength is rooted in self-respect, clarity, and intentional presence. When you lead from within, rather than through performance or comparison, you create space, stability, and inspiration for others to do the same. This chapter explores how subtle influence, grounded energy, and quiet confidence are often the most impactful forces in the room.

Reflect

Reflection invites you to examine where your leadership energy is coming from. Is it internal alignment or external validation? In moments of tension, subtle competition, or self-doubt, how do you show up? True strength doesn't chase approval; it anchors in purpose and self-trust.

- In social or professional spaces, ask if you're leading through grounded presence or a need to prove.
- Consider if you feel secure in your worth or subtly seek validation through performance.
- Reflect on experiences of quiet competition, especially with peers or same-gender dynamics. Did it lead to disconnection or deeper insight?

Journaling Prompt: *When have I felt the need to prove myself and what might change if I trusted I was already enough?*

Reframe

Reframing allows you to see that real influence comes from being intentional, not impressive. Competing for attention is a symptom of disconnection from self-worth. The most powerful people often speak less and listen more, because their presence speaks volumes on its own.

- You don't need to compete when you respect yourself, your calm is your magnetism.
- Leadership is rooted in alignment, not applause.
- When insecurity arises, choose presence over performance. Let generosity replace comparison.

Empowering Question: *Am I leaking energy trying to be seen or standing in my truth, quietly and completely?*

Reconnect

Reconnection is about returning to your most grounded, intentional self, especially when the room feels charged. Quiet strength doesn't shrink, but it doesn't shout either. Through daily practices, you can cultivate a steady, powerful presence that influences without effort.

- **Choose Your Energy Before You Enter the Room**
  Ask: "How do I want to be experienced today?" Choose one word calm, magnetic, wise and let your presence align.

- **Practice Listening as Leadership**
  Let silence be your strength. Deep, present listening often creates more impact than speaking first or loudest.

- **Compliment and Affirm**
  In moments of tension or comparison, offer sincere affirmation. This shifts the energy toward connection and trust.

- **Become the Brand of Your Future Self**
  What values do you carry? What feeling do you leave behind? Let every interaction reflect who you're becoming.

- **Release the Need to Impress**
  The right people will feel your clarity. Show less. Be more. Let presence replace performance.

Affirmation: *I lead with clarity, speak with intention, and influence through grounded presence.*

Final Thought: True Power Needs No Proof

Real influence isn't loud.
It doesn't hustle for attention or compete for approval.

It stands quietly in its truth.
It leads by example, not by ego.

When you no longer need to be the most important,
you become the most respected.
When you release comparison,
you create connection.

Grace disarms.
Humility magnetizes.
Presence commands without a word.

The woman rooted in self-respect
is unshakable,
not because she dominates,
but because she embodies peace.

This is Sovereign Living.

WHITE SPACE TO CLOSING THE GAP

"White space is to be regarded as an active element, not a passive background."
~Jan Tschichold

In both design and business, the white space, the space in between, is where the greatest opportunity lives. It is not merely the empty room on a page or an opening in your schedule. It is the quiet pause where inspiration whispers, the unmet need waiting for expression, the unseen possibility asking to be brought to life.

Most people focus on what is already visible, what is built, defined, or proven. But true leaders, creatives, and visionaries look deeper. They sense the potential hidden in the unseen, the idea waiting to be nurtured into form. They do not see what is missing as lack, but as invitation. White space becomes a bridge between what exists and what could be, a fertile ground for innovation, expansion, and soulful creation.

White space is not emptiness. It is presence. It is where the heart and mind meet possibility and where the most powerful breakthroughs emerge not from doing more but from allowing more. When we learn to pause, listen, and honor the quiet in-between, we close the gap between intention and inspiration, strategy and soul.

My Story: Seeing Gaps, Building Bridges

After my father's stage four colorectal cancer surgery and recovery, I was finally ready to step back into my professional life. The timing was serendipitous. A consulting project arrived through a former colleague and a trusted friend from my Unilever PLC days. It was a meaningful assignment, and something deep within me whispered yes.

Before I began, our family took a Caribbean cruise. It was joyful, simple, and pure. I watched my children with their sun-kissed faces and ice-cream-sticky fingers, and I felt my presence returning. Energy returning. Joy returning. I came home renewed and clear, carrying a sense of gratitude that reached far beyond rest.

One night, standing alone on the deck beneath a canopy of stars, the vision revealed itself. My work was not just about marketing or strategy. My true gift was in seeing the gaps, the unmet needs, the spaces between, and helping others bridge them. That realization awakened a new purpose.

With that clarity, my next creation was born: Closing the Gap. It was more than a consulting company; it was a mission and a calling to notice what others overlooked, to weave strategy with soul, and to transform the invisible into impact. From that vision, the business grew naturally, fueled by referrals, relationships, and results. Every client became a collaboration, every project a bridge. Because when you meet an authentic need with heart and integrity, growth is not something you chase. It flows, just like the space it was born from.

Turning Gaps into Gateways

What feels like absence may, in truth, be an invitation. The gap between what is and what could be is not a void to fear, but a threshold to possibility. Within that space lives your calling, the quiet knowing that something greater is asking to take form through you.

When you stop trying to fill the silence with noise and begin to listen for what only you can hear, direction begins to emerge. The pause becomes purpose. The unseen becomes sacred design.

You are not here to do everything. You are here to bridge what matters, to transform the distance between vision and reality into a living expression of grace.

Reflect

Reflection is about becoming aware of the spaces between the subtle tensions, the unseen needs, and the moments that feel incomplete. These gaps aren't failures; they're invitations. Often, what feels like something missing is your intuition sensing a place where your voice, skill, or insight is uniquely needed.

- Identify any areas in your life or work where something feels "off" or missing, even if you can't fully name it yet.

- Recall times you've noticed a disconnect between what's being offered and what's truly needed. What did you instinctively sense?

- Think back to a moment when a pause, gap, or uncertainty led you to clarity or reinvention. How did that space serve you?

Journaling Prompt: *Where in my life do I sense a gap and what might be possible if I stepped toward it instead of away from it?*

Reframe

Reframing invites you to see the white space not as a lack, but as a launchpad. The world often rewards what's loud and polished, but quiet gaps are where some of the most powerful ideas are born. Your ability to notice the unspoken, the underserved, or the unseen is not random, it's visionary.

- Gaps are not evidence of failure. They are proof that something new is ready to emerge.
- Your intuitive awareness, your way of seeing systems or sensing need, is a deeply strategic strength.
- You don't need to solve everything. Focus on one gap you can meaningfully bridge and let that be enough.

Empowering Question: *What do I naturally notice that others overlook and what impact could I create by responding to it?*

Reconnect

Reconnection turns your insight into intentional action. When you claim your unique lens and use it to serve a specific need, you move from scattered effort to Sovereign contribution. The gap you see may be exactly what you're here to fill, not through force, but through quiet, consistent leadership.

- **Conduct a Gap Audit**
  In any area of your life, ask: "What's missing?" "What's not being addressed?" "What's needed but overlooked?"

- **Identify Your Unique Lens**
  What do you see with ease that others don't? What are you constantly thanked for noticing or improving?

- **Clarify the Problem You Solve**
  Don't just offer skills. Offer answers to real, human needs. Define your niche by the pain point you resolve.

- **Take Action; Even If It's Small**
  Propose a new solution. Volunteer to bridge a process. Build something that fills a need, even if no one's asked yet.

- **Trust the Quiet Ideas**
  Innovation often begins in silence, not in the spotlight. Respect what comes to you when you're alone, listening.

Affirmation: *I honor what I uniquely see and I lead by bridging the gaps that call me forward.*

Final Thought: Step Boldly Into the Gap

White space is not wasted space.
It's potential.
It's peace.
It's the quiet before creation.

It's where clarity lives.
Where innovation is born.
Where purpose takes shape and path becomes clear.

Don't rush to fill the silence; listen to it.
Don't fear the gap; follow it.

Because the space between where you are
and where you're meant to be
is sacred ground for growth.

See the gap.
Bridge the gap.
Be the light that connects what's missing.

This is Sovereign Living.

FIXED MINDSET TO GROWTH MINDSET

"In a growth mindset, challenges are exciting rather than threatening."
~ Carol S. Dweck

Every transformation begins in the mind. The way we interpret failure, challenge, and potential quietly shapes the trajectory of our lives. A fixed mindset anchors us to what has been, to the belief that our abilities are static and our limits are permanent. A growth mindset, on the other hand, invites movement. It is the inner permission to evolve, to learn, to stumble, and still continue forward. It's not about being the best; it's about becoming willing to try again, knowing that effort itself is the path to expansion.

Shifting from a fixed to a growth mindset is not a one-time decision; it's a daily practice of awareness. It begins when we notice the quiet voice that says "I can't" and choose to ask, "What if I could?" It's in those small moments of resistance, when we reach for the unfamiliar, speak up instead of staying silent, or attempt what once felt out of reach, that our minds begin to rewire possibility. Growth isn't loud or instant; it's the steady accumulation of courage disguised as effort.

To move into a growth mindset is to trade judgment for curiosity and perfection for presence. It's recognizing that failure is not the opposite of success but the foundation of mastery. When we stop labeling ourselves and start learning ourselves, life expands. Every challenge becomes less about proving who we are and more about discovering who we're still becoming.

Psychologist Carol Dweck reminds us that growth begins not in mastery, but in how we meet the gap itself:

What is a **Growth Mindset**:

- Abilities and talents can be developed.
- Challenges are opportunities, not dead ends.
- Persistence matters more than innate talent.

By contrast, a **Fixed Mindset** whispers:

- "This is just who I am."
- "If I fail, it means I'm a failure."
- "If I'm not naturally good at something, why bother?"

One mindset closes the door. The other swings it wide open.

My Story: Stretching Beyond Self-Imposed Limits

I didn't always understand mindset, but I lived its impact. For years, I labeled myself: not good at math, not a numbers person, not tech-savvy. Those phrases were more than passing thoughts; they became self-fulfilling prophecies, invisible walls that limited how I showed up in both business and life. I mistook comfort for capability and repetition for truth, never realizing that my words were quietly shaping my reality.

Then came a defining moment. I had just launched my consulting company and was preparing my first quarterly financial review. My accountant was out sick, and I needed to present the data to a new client. Normally, I would have panicked or immediately outsourced the task. But something inside me whispered, *Try*. I opened the spreadsheet, watched a tutorial, and spent the afternoon learning formulas I had always avoided.

Was it messy? Yes. Did it take twice as long as it should have? Absolutely. But when I finished, I felt pride, not fear. That small victory rewired my self-talk. It reminded me that confidence is rarely built in comfort. It grows in the quiet moments when we choose curiosity over avoidance, effort over excuses, and presence over perfection.

Motherhood, reinvention, and entrepreneurship have each stretched me beyond the stories I once believed about myself. I've learned that fear is not a stop sign but a Compass pointing toward expansion. Every time I've leaned into what scared me, I've discovered a strength that had been waiting all along. The fear was never proof of incapacity. It was proof of possibility.

Choosing Progress Over Perfection

A fixed mindset says, "This is who I am." A growth mindset says, "This is who I'm becoming." The moment you stop expecting perfection and start valuing process, you unlock your ability to grow beyond what you thought was possible. Cultivating a growth mindset is not about blind optimism, it's about honoring your capacity to evolve, adapt, and rise with each challenge you meet.

Reflect

Reflection helps you uncover the stories you've told yourself about your capabilities and begin to challenge them. What you once labeled as a weakness may simply be a skill you haven't nurtured yet. The gap between fear and confidence is often just time, patience, and a willingness to begin again.

- Identify one area where you've told yourself, "I'm just not good at that." What belief is beneath that statement?
- Recall a past moment when you pushed through fear, learned something new, and came out stronger.
- Ask yourself: "Am I criticizing myself for not mastering something I've only just started?"

Journaling Prompt: *Where have I believed I wasn't capable and what would change if I saw myself as someone who can learn anything with time?*

Reframe

Reframing invites you to shift from limitation to possibility. A growth mindset isn't about pretending everything is easy, it's about choosing language and thought patterns that keep you open to learning. The way you speak to yourself creates the conditions for expansion or for stagnation.

- Trade fixed thoughts for flexible ones. "I'm not tech-savvy" becomes "I'm learning how to use tech more effectively."
- Replace "This is too hard" with "I haven't mastered this yet."

- View mistakes not as failures, but as feedback. Every misstep carries a lesson that brings you closer to growth.

Empowering Question: *What does this challenge reveal about the person I'm becoming?*

Reconnect

Reconnection turns new beliefs into lived experience. Growth mindset isn't a one-time shift, it's a daily practice. Through intention, action, and the right community, you can rewire your responses to discomfort and create momentum in any area you once felt stuck.

- **Flip the Script**
  Identify a limiting belief and reframe it:
  – Old: "I'm not creative."
  – New: "Creativity grows with practice and I'm practicing."

- **Collect Evidence of Growth**
  List three past moments when you grew through challenge. Let those memories remind you of your resilience.

- **Set a Stretch Goal**
  Choose one goal just outside your comfort zone and commit to learning through it. Progress happens on the edge.

- **Surround Yourself with Expanders**
  Be around those who challenge your thinking, support your growth, and celebrate your becoming, not just your results.

- **Celebrate Progress, Not Perfection**
  Every try counts. Acknowledge the effort, not just the outcome. This is how momentum is built.

Affirmation: *I grow with every step I take. I am capable, evolving, and becoming more than I once believed possible.*

Final Thought: You Are Becoming

A fixed mindset says, "This is it."
A growth mindset whispers,
"This is just the beginning."

You are not stuck; you are shifting.
You are not behind; you are unfolding.

Every challenge is an invitation.
Every stumble is sacred instruction.
Every step forward, no matter how small,
is evolution in motion.

Growth isn't about being the best.
It's about becoming the most *alive*, the most *awake*,
the most fully expressed version of you.

Progress is not linear; it's living, breathing expansion.
And it always begins right where you are.
Here. Now.

Keep becoming.
Keep growing.

This is Sovereign Living.

Part Three

HOME

WHERE ENERGY LIVES, DREAMS ARE BUILT & LEGACIES BEGIN

Home is more than a place. It is a reflection of your inner world. It holds your history, your habits, and your hopes. To reclaim your Compass at home is to turn your dwelling into a sanctuary, into a space that restores your energy and amplifies your purpose.

In **Home to Sacred Space**, you reimagine the home as an sanctuary, where every object and room holds intention. **Selling a Home to Selling an Investment** teaches that real estate is both practical and intentional, a conversation between foundation and expansion. **Selling One Investment to Unlock a Greater One** reminds you that letting go is how we grow; releasing one season makes room for another.

Through **Asset to 1031 Exchange** and **Renting to Buying,** you discover the balance between security and possibility. You learn to move resources with wisdom, not fear. **Land to Legacy** invites you to see property not as possession, but as stewardship of the ground beneath you and as a living partner in your Sovereignty.

Home, in its truest form, is both anchor and launchpad. It is a mirror of your evolution, a container for your peace, and a daily reminder that prosperity begins where you live.

HOME TO SACRED SPACE

"Arranging a home to hold happiness in place is the primary goal of Feng Shui."
~ Terah Kathryn Collins

Is your home your peaceful sanctuary, or simply a place to sleep, eat, and store your things? The spaces we inhabit quietly shape how we think, feel, and connect with ourselves and with life. As a realtor, I've walked into countless homes and can sense within moments whether a space feels inviting and alive or heavy and disconnected. A well-loved home radiates warmth and authenticity; a neglected one feels cold, no matter how luxurious its design. You can't fake energy. You either nurture it, or you don't.

Over the years, I've learned that a home is more than a reflection of style; it is a mirror of the soul. Through conscious choices, calming colors, curated artwork, intentional lighting, and meaningful placement, we create environments that invite stillness, gratitude, and renewal. A peaceful space doesn't arise by chance; it is built through daily care, mindful order, and an understanding of energy as a living presence.

Transforming a house into sacred space begins with intention. When you fill your surroundings with beauty, simplicity, and objects that carry meaning, you awaken harmony. You create a refuge for your spirit, a place where you can exhale and return to your true center. You deserve a home that not only shelters your body but also nourishes your light.

My Story: From a Mini Manse in the Woods to a Pied-à-Terre by the Sea

I grew up in a practical home near our church and school, surrounded by other Italian immigrant families. My sister and I shared a bedroom for almost twenty years, which meant plenty of sharing and plenty of squabbling over clothes and cosmetics. My parents would yell at us at least once a week to "clean up that mess!" The dresser top was sticky with hairspray from taming our teased hair, high heels were scattered across the floor like booby traps, and our poor closet organizer never stood a chance against the avalanche of clothes we stuffed inside.

Twelve years later, married with three children, I found myself in my dream home: a four-bedroom center-hall colonial with one bedroom for each child, a bonus room for a home office, and the pièce de résistance was an expansive living room and kitchen with a fireplace. The house sat gracefully on two manicured acres. When my parents visited, they would shake their heads and ask, "Why couldn't you keep your bedroom as clean as this house?"

By then, I had quietly begun studying the art of Feng Shui. Every room was approached with intention. Deep jewel-toned wall colors were chosen for elegance and balance, furniture was arranged in harmony with the space, and artwork was placed with reverence. Every cabinet, drawer, and even the refrigerator was meticulously organized. My children's VHS tapes and books were alphabetized. I was Marie Kondo before Marie Kondo became a household name. Organization wasn't just an aesthetic for me; it was a system of clarity and calm, one that allowed my children and nanny to find anything easily while I worked. It worked for me, and it worked for them.

After my divorce, I downsized to a smaller home. This time, the palette was unified, a warm, creamy off-white throughout. The furniture and artwork were quietly placed. The drawers and cabinets were still organized, but there was simply less. Less stuff. Less noise. More space to breathe.

When my youngest daughter graduated, I followed a long-held dream and moved to Fairfield, the beach town we had loved for years. My new home was less than a thousand square feet, elevated on stilts above the sand, with two bedrooms, sunlight pouring in, and ocean air filling every corner. Scaling down from two thousand square feet to one thousand required courage and clarity. I asked myself, *How am I going to scale back?* But it turned out to be simple. I kept only what the new space could hold: clothes, kitchenware, a few pieces of furniture and a few treasures. Everything else I sold, donated, or gave away.

What began as a practical necessity became a spiritual practice. The freedom of letting go was liberating. I learned the art of less is more.

Soon after, a job opportunity moved me to another beach in Malibu. My new home, a small pied-à-terre near the sea, is about eight hundred square feet. The space is entirely monochromatic, ivory and black, with artwork providing the only color. The energy is serene. My view includes the ocean on one side and a castle perched on a nearby hill on the other.

In the center of my living room sits an altar, a simple arrangement of intentional beauty. A pure white candle. Crystals that radiate calm. A heart-shaped glass from Quebec, inscribed with my name. Two glass blocks etched with the words *HEAL* and *SOUL.* And at the heart of it all, a small white marble Buddha I found at Two Buttons in the spring of 2015, about one year before leaving Connecticut for Southern California.

For those who know Elizabeth Gilbert and her book *Eat Pray Love*, Two Buttons was a spacious warehouse filled with Balinese imports, a venture Elizabeth Gilbert co-created with the man she met (and later married) during the "love" era of her book. Already an importer, they established the store in the United States so they could share his world of artistry and culture together. It was more than a retail space; it was a bridge between their two lives and the place where love met livelihood. That story captivated me, not just the romance, but the courage to burn down what was no longer true and begin again. The Buddha I brought home from that store is now my daily reminder: *Be courageous. Stand in your truth.*

Friends and family who visit my home always say the same thing: "It's so peaceful here." That's exactly my intention. Each move taught me something sacred: our spaces evolve as we do. What once required control became an invitation to clarity. What once defined success became an expression of serenity. A home is not simply where we live; it's where our energy lives. The more I simplified, the more peace I found. Every object I kept became intentional. Every space I curated became an act of self-honor. Creating a sacred home, I discovered, isn't about style or status. It's about aligning your outer world with your inner truth.

The Power of Energy and Environment

We often focus on mindset and emotions, but your environment is equally critical. Where you live, rest, and create either nourishes your soul or depletes it.

I've worked in creative agencies brimming with aliveness and in corporate offices where the fluorescent buzz felt like a slow leak of spirit. The same holds true for your home. Every color, sound, object, and person within it either raises or lowers your frequency.

Sacred Spaces Sell, Too

When preparing a home for sale, I guide clients through clearing, elevating, and re-staging the space.

We remove clutter. Add fresh plants and beautiful textures. Sometimes we fully stage the home, because buyers, like all of us, respond emotionally, not just intellectually.

According to the National Association of Realtors, 82% of buyer agents say staging helps buyers visualize a property as their future home. Staging isn't about furniture. It's about energy.

Creating a Sacred Home

Creating a sacred home isn't about perfection or price, it's about intention, energy, and flow. Your home is more than where you live; it's a living reflection of who you are. Every object, color, scent, and sound carries vibration, shaping how you feel and what you attract. When you infuse your space with care, clarity, and presence, you transform it from a container of things into a sanctuary for your soul.

Reflect

Reflection invites you to look at your home as a mirror of your inner landscape. The state of your environment reveals the state of your energy. Ask yourself:

- "Does my home feel alive, peaceful, and aligned, or heavy, cluttered, and disconnected?"
- "Which spaces restore me, and which silently drain me?"
- "If my home could speak, what would it say about how I'm living and loving myself?"

Focus: *When you pause to notice the energy of your space, the air, the light, the sounds, and the flow, you begin to see not only where you live but how you live.*

Reframe

Reframing invites you to recognize your home as a living sanctuary, an extension of your presence that holds, heals, and amplifies your essence.

- **Intention Over Perfection**
  A sacred home isn't about aesthetics or expense. It's about energy, rhythm, and how each object supports your peace.

- **Design as Energy Medicine**
  The placement of a bed, the presence of plants, the use of color, and the balance of elements are all tools to realign your home's vibration with your soul's truth.

- **Beauty as Spiritual Practice**
  A candle, a flower, or a thoughtfully curated corner

can remind your nervous system that you are safe, supported, and worthy of serenity.

Mantra: *My home reflects my wholeness. I tend to my space as I tend to my soul, with love, clarity, and care.*

Your home is not static; it breathes with you. When you infuse it with mindfulness, it becomes a sanctuary that nourishes your body, mind, and spirit.

Reconnect

Reconnection invites you to move from concept to practice, creating tangible rituals that honor your space and sustain sacred energy in daily life.

- **Clear & Cleanse**
  Open windows weekly. Let fresh air and natural light flow through. Burn sage, diffuse essential oils, or ring a bell to release stagnant energy.

- **Curate Intentionally**
  Keep only what holds purpose, beauty, or emotional resonance. Let go of what weighs down your energy or distracts your peace.

- **Harmonize with Nature**
  Bring in elements of earth, water, wood, fire, and metal to balance your environment. Fresh flowers, a bowl of stones, or a candle can transform the vibration of a room.

- **Bless Your Threshold**
  Each time you enter your home, pause and set an intention: *May this space hold peace, prosperity, and protection.*

- **Tend to Sound**
  Play soft music, open to birdsong, or rest in

silence. Let sound become a healing current that recalibrates your nervous system.

Affirmation: *I am the keeper of my home's energy. Each act of care is a prayer that anchors peace, beauty, and light.*

Final Thought: The Sacred Mirror of Home

Your home is not just where you live,
it's where your energy breathes.
It absorbs your moods, reflects your growth,
and mirrors your inner peace.

Every color is a frequency.
Every object carries memory.
Every corner whispers a story of who you've been,
and who you are becoming.

When you clear your space, you clear your mind.
When you bless your home, you bless your life.

Make beauty your prayer.
Let stillness be your design.
Infuse every room with presence, not perfection,
with meaning, not noise.

Because a sacred home doesn't just shelter you,
it expands you.

This is Sovereign Living.

Pro Tip:

Separate Work From Rest
If you work remotely, keep your workspace distinct from your bedroom. Energy lingers and you deserve a place of pure restoration, free from professional demands.

SELLING A HOME TO SELLING AN INVESTMENT

"A home is a space where memories are created, thus a relationship is developed. Homes are like relationships some you keep, some you grow from."
~ **Laura Alfano**

Selling a home is never just a financial decision; it's a deeply human one. Whether prompted by a life transition, an expansion, or an investment strategy, the process requires both practicality and presence. It invites you to honor what has held you while opening yourself to what is ready to unfold.

Each sale carries its own rhythm, a blend of logic and intuition, numbers and emotion, paperwork and prayer. To sell with intention is to recognize the energetic exchange at play: a release of old energy, a clearing of space, and a quiet invitation for new alignment to take root.

When approached consciously, selling becomes more than a transaction; it becomes a ritual of renewal. It's not about losing something familiar but about creating space for what's meant to grow next. Every closing is a quiet act of courage, a chance to express gratitude for what was, and to step forward with grace toward what's becoming.

My Story: Letting Go to Grow Forward

I was inspired to become a real estate agent in my thirties, though I didn't begin until my fifties. For most of my career, I worked in corporate marketing, a world where knowing your product was everything. When I began buying and selling homes, I was surprised by how many agents lacked that same depth of understanding. I remember walking through properties, asking thoughtful questions, and hearing, "Oh, I'll have to get back to you," followed by silence.

Years later, when it came time to sell my own condo in Naples, FL, I finally met an agent who changed everything. He listened, advised, and acted with precision and care. While I was an out-of-state owner-seller and couldn't handle the logistics myself, he coordinated every detail, cleaning, furniture removal, and staging, and sold the property to an all-cash buyer who had been quietly waiting for the right home.

That sale was emotional. The condo had been our second home, a gathering place for holidays, laughter, and family memories. Letting it go felt like closing a chapter of my life. I remember walking through one last time, the rooms echoing with the energy of every meal, every milestone, every quiet Sunday morning. But when the offer came through, I knew in my heart it was the right decision.

The proceeds became the foundation for something new: my beach house in Fairfield, CT, a long-held dream. It was proof that endings, when approached with grace, can become powerful beginnings. Ten years later, in a beautiful twist of fate, my mother purchased a home in Naples, in a nearby neighborhood where I once sold that condo. Now new memories around the holidays are being created with my family and the nostalgia from the years past, remain.

That experience taught me something lasting. Every sale holds a story, and every ending creates space for the next beginning. Letting go, when done with faith and gratitude, is never a loss. It is a realignment.

Releasing One Home to Welcome Another

Selling a home isn't simply a financial exchange; it's a spiritual one. It is the art of releasing a space that has held your history so you can step into one that will hold your future. Whether your move is inspired by growth, simplicity, or new opportunity, the process asks for both strategy and surrender.

When approached with clarity, gratitude, and vision, selling becomes less about letting go and more about making room for expansion, freedom, and the next chapter of your Sovereign life.

Reflect

Reflection invites you to look beyond the surface details of selling and into the deeper meaning of release. Ask yourself:

- What am I truly letting go of? The structure, or the story within it?
- Which memories am I ready to carry forward, and which can I leave behind with gratitude?

- Does this move represent freedom, growth, or healing and how can I honor that truth?

Focus: *Every home holds energy, just as every chapter does. Before you list or pack, pause to bless the space that sheltered you. Walk room by room, remembering what it gave you: laughter, lessons, love, and thank it before you leave.*

Reframe

Reframing allows you to transform the selling process from a transaction into a practice of intention and Sovereignty.

- **Choose Alignment Over Urgency**
  The best time to sell isn't when you *must*, but when you're *ready*. When you act from readiness, you sell from strength.

- **Partner with Integrity**
  The right agent is not just a salesperson but a trusted advisor, someone who aligns with your values, communicates clearly, and represents your story with care.

- **Price with Wisdom, Not Emotion**
  Let the market guide you, not nostalgia. Pricing is an energetic statement of value, yours and your home's.

- **Present with Purpose**
  Staging is more than strategy; it's an offering. Each room can tell a story of peace, beauty, and possibility for its next owner.

Mantra: *I release with gratitude and prepare with grace. What I once called home becomes a sacred gift for someone new.*

Reconnect

Reconnection calls you to step into your next chapter with confidence and clarity and to see selling not as an ending, but as a recalibration of your path.

- **Sell from Strength**
  When you move by choice rather than circumstance, you act from empowerment. You set terms, pace, and priorities that align with your peace.

- **Explore Quietly if Needed**
  Sovereignty means choice, including the choice for discretion. You can sell quietly, exploring off-market opportunities that honor your privacy.

- **Reinvest with Intention**
  The equity you unlock isn't just financial, it's energetic. Direct it toward spaces, experiences, or investments that expand your sense of purpose and possibility.

- **Bless the Transition**
  Before closing, pause to bless both homes, the one you're leaving and the one awaiting you. Energy travels with intention; send it forward with love.

Affirmation: *I sell with wisdom, not urgency. I move with intention, not fear. Every transition expands my freedom and deepens my peace.*

Final Thought: Excellence Is in the Execution

Selling a home is never just a transaction,
it's a translation of energy, emotion, and intention.

Partner with integrity.
Price with wisdom.
Present with heart and elegance.

Because excellence isn't luck, it's alignment.
It's the fusion of clarity and care,
strategy and soul.

When you lead with intention,
every detail becomes an act of respect,
for the home, for the client,
for the story being completed.

And when those elements harmonize,
the result is not merely a sale,
but a seamless celebration of what was,
and an open invitation to what's next.

This is Sovereign Living.

SELLING ONE INVESTMENT TO UNLOCK A GREATER ONE

"Ninety percent of all millionaires become so through owning real estate."
~ *Andrew Carnegie*

Sometimes, the most strategic time to sell is when you don't need to. When you're not pressed for time or resources, you stand in a position of strength, able to make clear, confident, values-driven decisions that open the door to greater opportunities.

Selling without pressure isn't about loss; it's about liberation. It is the art of releasing something good to make room for something greater. It's about trusting that timing is not just financial but spiritual. The most aligned transactions don't happen in haste; they happen in harmony. When clarity meets calm, the results often exceed expectation.

Selling from stillness invites you to make decisions from expansion, not contraction, from vision, not fear. It allows you to move beyond survival thinking into strategic creation. In this space, you're not chasing opportunity; you're choosing it.

My Story: Selling in Stillness, Gaining in Grace

During the Covid-19 pandemic, real estate agents were deemed essential workers. At first, I found it absurd. We weren't saving lives. But soon, I realized that home *was* saving lives. People were seeking comfort, safety, and change.

As interest rates dropped and inventory vanished, I watched homeowners in Malibu make bold, intentional moves. Some sold family properties they had held for decades, not out of urgency but out of curiosity: *What if we could do something different?*

One family listed their coastal estate at an aspirational price, expecting nothing. It sold in less than thirty days at full asking price. With remote work and school, they packed up, drove cross-country, and spent time with loved ones. Eventually, they reinvested in a larger property on the Connecticut shoreline, close to family, surrounded by land, and with significant financial freedom from their sale.

Another couple, empty nesters with grown children, sold their ocean-view home to fund a new chapter abroad. Their move wasn't driven by need; it was fueled by possibility. They spent a year living in Europe, exploring cultures they had always dreamed of, investing the rest wisely for generational impact.

What began as uncertainty became Sovereignty. They didn't sell out of pressure; they sold from peace. They created choice, and choice is the purest form of wealth.

From Equity to Expansion: The Power of Perspective

Selling a home can be emotional, but when done consciously, it is also transformational. Every sale creates a ripple, freeing equity, shifting energy, and making space for new beginnings.

Whether you are downsizing, reinvesting, or relocating, this chapter invites you to reflect, reframe, and reconnect. See selling not as an ending, but as an elegant act of evolution, a conscious transition that opens new pathways for growth, alignment, and deeper peace within yourself and your surroundings.

Reflect

Reflection reveals the difference between attachment and alignment. Sometimes what you're clinging to is simply ready to grow into its next form.

Before deciding to sell, pause and ask yourself:

- "Am I holding this property out of habit, comfort, or purpose?"
- "What would financial and emotional freedom look like in my next chapter?"
- "If I released this home, what could it open space for, peace, proximity, possibility?"

Journaling Prompt: *What could unfold if I trusted that letting go is not loss, but an invitation to rise into my next level of freedom?*

Reframe

Reframing turns selling into strategy.

- Selling from strength is not loss, it's leverage.
- The goal is not to escape a home, but to expand your life.
- Freedom is the ability to move when *you* choose, not when circumstance demands it.

When you sell consciously, you aren't letting go; you're trading stagnation for flow, comfort for clarity, and certainty for potential. That's not risk; that's renewal.

Mantra: *I sell from peace, not pressure. I release what has served its purpose and make room for what's ready to grow.*

Reconnect

Reconnect with what truly matters.

- Revisit your long-term goals, financial, personal and spiritual.
- Partner with an advisor who understands your values as much as your valuation.
- Explore your options with curiosity, not urgency.

Affirmation: *I release with gratitude, knowing that what I free will return to me in new, abundant form. Every sale is a seed for my next season of growth.*

Explore Quietly, Sell Strategically

Not quite ready to go public? Consider a discreet, private exclusive, off-market offering. This approach allows your agent to quietly introduce your home to a curated network of qualified buyers. It gives you the flexibility to test the market, gauge interest, and entertain offers without the pressure or exposure of a full public listing.

When privacy, discretion, and control are priorities, an off-market strategy offers the best of all worlds. You remain in charge of timing and visibility while allowing the right opportunity to find you. It is a refined, intentional way to sell, anchored in confidence, not urgency and often leads to more aligned and meaningful transactions.

Final Thought: Choice Is the Ultimate Luxury

The best time to sell isn't when you must;
it's when you choose.

When you act from clarity instead of crisis,
selling becomes more than a transaction;
it becomes transformation.

Real wealth isn't measured in
square footage or returns.
It's measured in peace.
In presence.
In the freedom to decide your
next chapter on your own terms.

Choice is the highest form of abundance
the ability to move, create, and expand
without fear, without rush, without regret.

Letting go is not loss.
It's the quiet, powerful act of making room for more:
more alignment, more joy, more you.

This is Sovereign Living.

ASSET TO 1031 EXCHANGE

*"Price is what you pay.
Value is what you get."*
~ *Warren Buffett*

For the discerning investor, the goal is not just to grow wealth; it is to grow wisely. A Sovereign investor understands that prosperity is not measured only in numbers, but in the freedom, stability, and opportunity those numbers create.

The 1031 Exchange is one of the most strategic and underutilized tools for building long-term financial Sovereignty. It allows you to sell an investment property and reinvest the proceeds into another like-kind property, deferring capital gains taxes and allowing your equity to keep compounding rather than being diminished by taxation.

When done with foresight and alignment, a 1031 Exchange transforms a simple transaction into a powerful act of generational wealth stewardship. It is not just a move on a balance sheet; it is a declaration of legacy and long-term vision.

My Story: From Transaction to Transformation

I first learned about the 1031 Exchange not through a textbook, but through experience, the kind that humbles, refines, and teaches in equal measure. Years ago, when I sold an investment property, I was simply grateful for the proceeds and ready to move forward. What I did not yet understand was how that sale could have been leveraged to preserve and multiply the return through reinvestment.

Later, as I deepened my work in real estate, I began to recognize the profound potential of this strategy. When executed with timing, expert guidance, and patience, a 1031 Exchange can do more than defer taxes; it can extend the lifespan of wealth itself. It is not just a tool for saving money, it is a method for sustaining legacy and designing financial freedom.

One particular client stands out in my memory: a retired couple ready to simplify their lives and shift from active property management to passive income. Together, we executed a seamless 1031 Exchange, transitioning from three aging rental homes into a fractional interest in a Class A multifamily property. Within months, they were earning higher monthly income, enjoying tax-deferred growth, and traveling freely without the burden of tenant calls or repairs.

Over time, I have watched clients transform not only their portfolios, but their peace of mind. Some moved from multiple single-family rentals into streamlined, high-performing assets. Others transitioned into Delaware Statutory Trusts (DSTs) that provided steady income without the stress of hands-on management. Each success story reinforced the truth that financial decisions rooted in clarity and courage often lead to emotional and energetic liberation.

Wealth, like energy, is meant to flow. When you move your investments with intention, not from fear or haste, you invite expansion. True prosperity is never found in mere accumulation; it is found in alignment, where money, purpose, and peace coexist in balance and grace.

Supercharge Your Investment Strategy with Intention

Before diving into the details of a 1031 Exchange, it's important to pause and recognize what this moment truly represents. Selling an investment property is not just a financial pivot; it is a moment of evolution. You are shifting energy from one form to another, allowing the value you have built to flow forward into new opportunities. Reflection turns this process from a transaction into a transformation. It ensures that your next investment not only grows your wealth but also expands your freedom, peace, and purpose.

Reflect

Reflection asks you to consider your relationship to both money and momentum. Before pursuing a 1031 Exchange, pause and ask:

- "What is my vision for wealth, not just in numbers, but in impact and freedom?"
- "Am I building equity for expansion, or clinging to assets out of comfort or fear of change?"
- "How can I use my investments not only to accumulate, but to create alignment and legacy?"

Empowering Question: *What would shift if I viewed every financial decision not as a transaction, but as a declaration of who I am becoming?*

Reframe

Reframing allows you to move from transactional thinking to transformational strategy.

- **See the 1031 Exchange as Expansion, Not Escape**
  You're not selling to leave something behind; you're evolving your portfolio toward greater freedom and possibility.

- **Let Your Money Work as Hard as You Do**
  By deferring taxes, you allow your equity to keep building momentum and turn past gains into future growth.

- **Think Generationally**
  A 1031 Exchange isn't only about you. With strategic planning, it can set the foundation for your heirs to inherit assets with a "stepped-up basis," minimizing or eliminating capital gains altogether.

- **Honor Timing as a Teacher**
  The 45- and 180-day windows of a 1031 Exchange teach patience and precision. These are not limitations; they are invitations to act with discipline, focus, and clarity.

Mantra: *I don't chase opportunity; I align with it. Every investment I make is a reflection of wisdom, purpose, and growth.*

Reconnect

Reconnection invites you to see your wealth as a living ecosystem, one that thrives when tended with both intelligence and intention.

- **Work with Trusted Guides**
  Surround yourself with a qualified intermediary and a CPA who understand the nuances of the 1031 exchange law and align with your long-term goals. Sovereign wealth is never built alone. It's built with wise counsel.

- **Diversify with Conscious Design**
  Reinvest in properties that align with your vision of lifestyle, legacy, and impact. Whether that's passive income, sustainability, or freedom from management, let your investments serve your evolution.

- **Anchor Wealth in Purpose**
  Ask not just "What can this asset earn?" but "What can this asset empower?" True prosperity supports your peace, your community, and your capacity to give.

- **Trust the Flow of Exchange**
  Just as you once released a home to step into another, each financial exchange mirrors a spiritual one; it is a letting go of what is complete to make room for what is meant.

Affirmation: *My wealth circulates with intention. I exchange fear for faith, pressure for purpose, and profit for possibility.*

Final Thought: Build Generational Wealth, One Exchange at a Time

Wealth is not what you keep; it's what you cultivate.
A 1031 Exchange is more than a strategy.
It's a bridge between seasons.
A continuation of purpose.

It allows your capital to move as you move,
flowing forward, evolving wisely,
multiplying meaning.
Each exchange is an act of stewardship,
a choice to preserve momentum rather than pause it.

When guided by clarity, care, and consciousness,
it becomes an elegant expression of Sovereignty.
A declaration that your wealth serves you,
not the other way around.

Direct your energy with purpose.
Invest with presence.
Build with intention.
And watch your legacy take root,
one exchange at a time.

This is Sovereign Living.

RENTING TO BUYING

"Buying real estate is not only the best way, the quickest way, the safest way, but the only way to become wealthy."
~ Marshall Field

Buying your first home is one of life's most rewarding milestones and one of its most strategic financial moves. Yet for many first-time buyers, the leap from renting to owning can feel overwhelming. Rising prices, competitive markets, and limited inventory can make homeownership seem out of reach.

But the truth is, most renters can afford the monthly costs of ownership; they simply need the right plan to get there. Preparation, partnership, and perspective are key. When you approach the process with clarity and confidence, buying your first home becomes more than an achievement; it becomes a declaration of stability, freedom, and long-term vision.

Homeownership is more than a financial transaction; it is a spiritual statement of belonging. It roots you in community, builds generational security, and invites you to invest not only in property but in possibility. Each key handed over represents not just a door unlocked, but a future expanded.

My Story: Turning a Renter into a Buyer

When I began my real estate career in Malibu, I didn't have a built-in network. My children weren't raised here, and most community groups already had preferred agents. So, I got creative.

One afternoon, a Pepperdine University parent I had helped find a rental introduced me to another family searching for off-campus housing during the height of COVID-19. After weeks of touring rental properties, I decided to pause and analyze the numbers. What would two years of rent cost compared to purchasing a small condo and collecting rent from roommates? I presented the side-by-side comparison, complete with projected costs, potential appreciation, and tax advantages.

The parents immediately saw the value. They purchased a beautifully updated condominium, allowing their student to live comfortably while building equity. That single transaction became the spark for several others. It also became a priceless life lesson for the student to understand what it takes to invest in real estate and become a landlord. Many of those families still own their properties today, some now held in family trusts as investments for their children's futures. The ripple effect was profound, both financially and personally.

That experience reminded me that every client interaction is an opportunity to educate, empower, and elevate. My role is not only to close deals but to expand vision. Real estate, when approached with strategy and heart, is more than ownership; it is the art of creating possibility, legacy, and long-term peace of mind.

Before You Begin: The Foundations of Financial Readiness

Owning a home starts with clarity. Evaluate your financial position honestly, not just what you earn, but what you keep, spend, and save.

- **Down Payment Options**
  While a conventional 20% is ideal, many programs allow much less. Explore FHA, VA, or first-time buyer incentives.

- **Strategic Family Support**
  Don't overlook family resources. Explore gifted funds, intra-family loans, or shared LLC ownership to help bridge the gap.

- **Budget with Vision**
  Include not just the purchase price but also taxes, insurance, HOA fees, and maintenance. Buy a home that supports your lifestyle, not one that restricts it.

A seasoned agent will help you translate these numbers into possibility, ensuring your home purchase enhances your life, not burdens it.

From Shelter to Sovereignty

A home is more than four walls; it is the physical embodiment of safety, self-worth, and stability. Renting offers flexibility, but buying invites you to root. It marks a shift from temporary to timeless, from dependence to ownership, not only of property but of personal direction.

Homeownership, when approached consciously, becomes a practice of Sovereignty. It calls you to commit to a place, to your vision, and to your next evolution. Every mortgage payment becomes an investment in your future self, and every key turned in a new lock a reminder that you built this.

This transition is not only about property; it is about presence. It is an act of grounding your worth in something lasting, a declaration that you are ready to live with both purpose and permanence.

Reflect

Before stepping into homeownership, take time to understand what this transition truly means for you.

- What does homeownership represent? Stability, freedom, legacy, or independence?
- Ask: "How do I want my home to feel, not just look?"
- Ask: "Am I buying to escape renting, or to align with the next chapter of my life?"

Reflection turns the search for a house into a search for alignment. The home you choose will not only hold your belongings, it will hold your energy, your dreams, and your direction.

Journal Prompt: *What does "home" mean to you, not just as a location, but as an expression of who you're becoming.*

Reframe

Reframing is where strategy meets mindset. Buying your first home isn't just about qualifying for a mortgage it's about qualifying for your next level of life.

- **From Renter to Investor**
  See your first home not just as shelter but as a launch pad for wealth. Even a small condo can become an appreciating asset or future rental.

- **From Emotion to Education**
  It's easy to get caught up in aesthetics. Focus instead on fundamentals such as location, structure, and growth potential.

- **From Fear to Foresight**
  Rising interest rates or competitive offers can trigger anxiety. Remember, you're not buying in a race; you're building for longevity.

- **From "Can I afford this?" to "How can I afford this?"**
  Reframe financial limitations as creative challenges. Gifted funds, shared ownership, or temporary adjustments in lifestyle can turn possibility into reality.

Mantra: *I am not just buying a home; I am building a foundation for freedom, stability, and future prosperity.*

Reconnect

Reconnection is about grounding the process in your greater vision. Once the paperwork and planning are in motion, return to the deeper why: your desire for rootedness, safety, and peace.

- **Choose Community Over Perfection**
  You can change a kitchen, but you can't change your neighborhood. Choose a location that nourishes your lifestyle and supports your values.

- **Prepare Emotionally**
  Buying a home is both exciting and vulnerable. Stay centered by seeking wise guidance and practicing patience.

- **Think Long-Term**
  Will this home still serve you in five or ten years? Can it grow with your needs or evolve into an investment property?

- **Trust Your Inner Compass**
  Walk through a home and listen, not just to your agent or your lender, but to your body. Does the space feel calm? Expansive? Grounded?

Affirmation: *I make financial decisions rooted in wisdom. My home is a reflection of the life I'm ready to live: stable, spacious, and Sovereign.*

Final Thought: Be Ready, Emotionally and Logistically

Buying a home is more than a milestone; it's a mirror.
It reflects your values, your vision,
your readiness to expand.

Preparation is not pressure; it's peace.
It's the art of aligning heart and strategy,
intuition and intention.

When you plan with clarity,
emotion becomes your Compass, not your captor.
When you act with wisdom,
each decision becomes an act of devotion.

You're not just acquiring property.
You're anchoring possibility.
You're choosing where your next chapter
will grow roots and gather light.

True wealth lives in readiness,
emotional, spiritual, and practical.
Because when you're aligned, doors open effortlessly.

Move with purpose.
Buy with faith.
Build from balance.

This is Sovereign Living.

LAND TO LEGACY

"The best investment on Earth is earth."
~ Louis Glickman

Home begins not only with a structure, but with the earth beneath it. Long before walls rise or gardens grow, land holds the first whisper of belonging. There's a silent promise of what could be. To invest in land is to invest in possibility itself.

For generations, owning land has been one of the most profound ways to build security, wealth, and lasting legacy. Land is more than an asset; it is permanence in a world that is constantly changing. It offers something no stock or digital currency ever can. It provides the grounding energy of place, the freedom to create, and the privilege to preserve a piece of the Earth itself.

Across cultures, owning land has always symbolized opportunity, independence, and future prosperity. Whether it's a family ranch, a vineyard in the hills, a coastal bluff, or a forested retreat, land endures. It holds stories. It invites new beginnings.

My Story: Turning Earth into a Family Legacy

Early in my career at a boutique real estate agency, I was introduced to a client seeking land in Malibu. I had little experience with land sales at the time, but I was eager to learn. The client, a dentist who had grown up in Japan and always dreamed of learning to surf, shared that he wanted to build a home with his sons near the beach and learn to surf together.

I found the perfect lot and immersed myself in every detail: zoning regulations, geological surveys, neighborhood history, architectural restrictions, and the long, complex permitting process. None of it deterred him. His dream was not about profit but about purpose. He wanted to create something lasting, a place his children could one day return to and say, "This is where it began."

I connected him with a local architect, and together they designed a home that honored both the land and the legacy he envisioned. Years later, he invited me to visit. The walls were adorned with photographs of famous surf breaks, the rooms filled with light and laughter. He and his sons still surf together, still beginners, but joyfully bonded by the earth they shaped with their own hands.

That experience reminded me that land is not just an investment. It is an inheritance of meaning, connection, and memory. A living symbol of care, patience, and devotion. Every foundation we help build becomes a story of belonging, a bridge between vision and legacy, and a promise carried forward through generations.

Land Is a Legacy Investment

Unlike structures that weather and wear, land appreciates with time and often at an accelerated pace in highly sought-after locations. Raw land offers a blank canvas for dreams yet to be realized, a chance to plant seeds today that future generations will harvest tomorrow.

Benefits of Owning Land:

- Lower entry costs compared to developed properties
- Complete creative freedom to build when ready, or simply hold
- Potential for significant long-term appreciation
- Emotional and spiritual connection to the land itself
- The opportunity to create a family legacy that transcends generations

Vision Yields Opportunity

In an increasingly crowded world, untouched land becomes more precious each year. While many shy away from purchasing raw land due to daunting permits, zoning, or development complexities, the savvy few recognize that vision creates value.

With expert guidance, navigating the intricacies of site planning, zoning regulations, utility access and environmental protections, you can transform a patch of raw earth into a dream realized, or an investment that matures like fine wine.

Malibu: Scarcity Meets Beauty

Consider Malibu, a world-renowned community along California's iconic coastline. Here, where ocean and sky meet seamlessly, parcels of raw land still exist, tucked along private ridgelines and canyon hillsides, as well as beach front. In Malibu, to own land is to hold something truly rare: a chance to craft a private sanctuary on or above the Pacific while participating in one of the world's most desirable real estate markets.

Whether building a modern architectural masterpiece, preserving a natural retreat, or holding for future generations, land in Malibu, like land anywhere iconic, becomes more valuable, more revered, and more irreplaceable with each passing year. Its beauty is not only visual but vibrational, reminding you that some places are meant to be experienced as both investment and inspiration.

Yet Malibu is just one example. Wherever your heart feels drawn, whether to the desert, the mountains, the coastline, or the wide open plains, land remains an invitation to dream, to design, and to dwell with intention. It is the meeting point of vision and belonging, where nature and legacy converge.

From Ground to Growth: A Moment of Reflection

Land asks something different of us than other investments. It asks for vision, patience, and reverence. When you invest in land, you aren't simply purchasing property, you are entering into a conversation with the Earth itself.

This is where **Sovereign Living** begins to merge the practical with the sacred. Whether you are buying your first parcel, preserving a family property, or dreaming of open acres yet to be built upon, this is your invitation to reflect, reframe, and reconnect to see land not just as ownership, but as legacy in motion.

Reflect

Before acquiring land, pause to listen to the land itself, not the market. Ask yourself:

- "What legacy do I want this piece of earth to hold?"
- "Am I seeking ownership, or am I seeking rootedness?"
- "How do I want this land to serve?" "Is it to create your dream home?" "Hold and preserve?" "Invest for future wealth?" "Craft a family compound?" "Support conservation efforts?"

Reflection is not about the transaction; it's about understanding your *why*. Land magnifies intention, so begin with clarity of purpose.

Empowering Question: *What if the land you choose is also choosing you, calling you to steward, shape and sustain something larger than yourself?*

Reframe

Reframing invites you to see land not just as property, but as partnership.

- Land is not something you simply own, it's something you steward.
- Value is not measured only in dollars, but in the energy, care, and legacy it carries.
- The best investors aren't just builders, they are visionaries who create meaning from the ground up.

When you reframe your perspective, you realize that every plot of land is a canvas for possibility. It becomes a physical manifestation of what you believe about abundance, creation, and contribution.

Mantra: *I am not an owner of land, but a steward of legacy. I build with reverence. I plant with purpose. I leave the Earth better than I found it.*

Reconnect

Reconnect by bringing reverence into your relationship with the earth.

- Walk the land before you buy it. Feel its energy. Listen to its story.
- Visualize what peace, family, or legacy might look like there.
- Treat your ownership as guardianship and an opportunity to preserve beauty, nurture life, and build something that endures beyond you.

Affirmation: *I honor the land as both foundation and teacher. What I build upon it will reflect not only who I am, but who I am becoming.*

Final Thought: Steward the Soil, Sustain the Soul

Land is not just where you stand;
it's what stands with you.
It remembers. It restores.
It rewards those who honor it.

To own land is to enter a sacred contract,
between body and earth, vision and time.
When you build, build with reverence.
When you plant, plant with faith.
When you sell, do so with gratitude
for what the soil has given.

True wealth isn't in the acreage you hold,
but in the intention you bring to it.

Be the kind of steward who listens before acting,
who leaves more than footprints,
who shapes legacy with love, not just labor.

Because the land beneath you is living wisdom
and you are part of its eternal story.

This is Sovereign Living.

Part Four

ETIQUETTE
A DEVOTIONAL PRACTICE OF ELEGANCE, PRESENCE & EMOTIONAL INTELLIGENCE

Etiquette is mindfulness expressed through movement, the quiet art of honoring life with presence and intention. It is not about rules, but about resonance, a daily devotion to grace, awareness, and alignment. Through it, we turn ordinary moments into sacred acts of respect and care.

In **Arriving Late to Being Early**, you rediscover time as devotion, showing up prepared, grounded, and in integrity. **Unprepared to Prepared** reminds you that readiness is reverence, a spiritual act that communicates, "You matter." These chapters teach that presence is power and that the woman who honors her own timing becomes magnetic, calm, capable, and deeply trustworthy. Elegance begins long before the door opens; it begins in how you prepare to arrive.

Disciplined to Devotional transforms structure into sacred rhythm, the daily doing that becomes an offering of heart. **Buying a Gift to Thoughtful Gift Giving** elevates generosity from transaction to tribute, turning simple gestures into echoes of love and legacy.

Together, they remind you that refinement is not about appearance but energy, the care you bring to what you create, give, and tend to. Sovereignty is not stern; it is soft strength expressed through intention.

Text or Email to Handwritten Note restores the lost intimacy of touch, where ink carries emotion and presence lingers beyond the screen. **Sorry to Excuse Me** invites you to speak with grounded confidence, exchanging apology for authenticity. Finally, **Apology to Appreciation** reframes relationships through gratitude, moving from fixing what is broken to celebrating what is whole.

When we elevate the act of **Eating to Dining,** we reclaim mealtime as a moment of beauty, intention, and connection. It becomes less about consumption and more about communion with our food, our company, and ourselves. In choosing presence over pace, we rediscover that true nourishment feeds both body and soul.

Etiquette is grace in motion, the quiet language of respect and presence that turns every moment into a reflection of love. It is how we move through life with intention, leaving behind a legacy of calm, kindness, and quiet strength.

ARRIVING LATE TO BEING EARLY

"Arriving late was a way of saying that your own time was more valuable than the time of the person who waited for you."
~ Karen Joy Fowler

Time is one of our most sacred currencies, and unlike money, we can't make more of it. When we show up late, we're not just delaying the moment; we're sending a message, whether we mean to or not.

Being early is more than a logistical habit. It's a mark of presence, respect, and readiness, especially in a world that runs on connection and commitment. Punctuality tells others: I value you. I value this moment. And I showed up for it.

True punctuality isn't about perfectionism or control. It's about creating energetic space. When you arrive early, you give yourself time to breathe, observe, and align. You become the calm before the collective rhythm begins. In business, in love, in life, the one who is centered first leads best.

My Story: Honor Time, Create Peace

In my professional world, I've learned to treat time like trust. It is earned and protected.

As a real estate agent, I make it a personal rule to arrive at showings early. Not just on time, but early enough to walk the property, adjust the lights, open windows, light candles, and mentally prepare. That quiet moment before a client walks in allows me to align my energy with the space. I've found it makes a difference, not only in the way clients feel but in the way I lead.

In my personal life, I haven't always been so exacting. Like many of us, I used to underestimate how long things would take: the drive, the parking, the time to walk from the car to the event, or to gather everything I needed before heading out.

One experience that stands out was a Sunday sporting event in Los Angeles. Friend A is the planner. He maps out parking, checks traffic, even notes restroom stops. He wanted to leave by 10:30 a.m. for a 1:00 p.m. game. Friend B is more spontaneous. "We'll be fine," she said. "Let's leave around 11:30."

On separate occasions, I tried both plans. With Friend A, we parked close, grabbed snacks, wandered into the stadium with ease, and even caught warm-ups. The whole experience felt grounded, intentional, and unrushed, as though the day had expanded for us. With Friend B, we hit traffic, circled for parking, arrived breathless and laughing, but with little time to settle or truly savor the moment.

Neither approach was wrong, but both created very different energetic states. And what I've learned is this: if you're someone who values peace, presence, or professionalism, being early isn't a personality trait. It's a form of love and respect.

Arriving Early as a Gift of Presence

In a culture that glorifies being busy and cutting it close, choosing to be early is a quiet revolution. It's not about control, it's about care. Mindful punctuality isn't just a sign of discipline; it's an offering of respect, intention, and grounded energy. When you show up early, you don't just honor the schedule, you honor the space, the people, and yourself.

Reflect

Reflection helps you explore your relationship with time and what your habits around arrival might be communicating, both to yourself and to others. Being chronically late isn't always about disorganization, it can also reflect avoidance, overstretching, or a lack of presence. Examining these patterns gently allows you to shift with awareness, not shame.

- Do you often find yourself rushing at the last minute? What impact does this have on your nervous system, relationships, or day?
- Think of someone in your life who values punctuality. How might your timing affect their experience of your care or presence?
- How do you feel when someone is consistently late? What message do you receive from their timing?

Journaling Prompt: *What message am I sending, to myself and others, by how I show up in time and space?*

Reframe

Reframing invites you to see timeliness not as obligation, but as an act of love. Early arrival is more than being prepared, it's being present. It creates room to breathe, reset, and arrive with grace. When you honor time as sacred, you naturally create more peace, not only for others, but for yourself.

- Being early is not just a habit, it's a devotion to care and presence.
- Early arrival creates space: for grounding, for connection, and for conscious leadership.
- Time is energy. How you honor someone else's time reflects how you value the relationship.

Mantra: *I arrive early to create space for intention, respect, and presence.*

Reconnect

Reconnection is the practice of choosing punctuality not from pressure, but from love. Through small, intentional shifts, you can transform arrival into ritual. Create a moment of stillness before you begin. When you treat time as sacred, you begin every interaction with mindfulness.

- **Choose One Area to Practice Mindful Punctuality**
  Select a single event this week, a meeting, school pickup, dinner, or phone call and commit to arriving early, intentionally.

- **Use Reminders and Buffers**
  Set alarms or calendar notifications ahead of time. Build in cushions so time serves you, not the other way around.

- **Prepare the Night Before**
  Lay out your outfit. Fill the gas tank. Gather your essentials. Morning clarity starts with evening intention.

- **Treat Early Arrival as a Gift**
  Use the extra time to pause, breathe, visualize, or say a quiet prayer of gratitude. Let it become a sacred prelude to the moment ahead.

Affirmation: *I arrive with intention. My presence begins before I speak and I offer it with care, not hurry.*

Final Thought: Arrive Early for the Life You Want to Live

Every minute holds meaning.
Every moment is an invitation.
When you arrive early,
you enter alignment with yourself,
with others,
with the rhythm of what's unfolding.

Early is not about control.
It's about presence.
It's about respect, for time, for trust, for connection.

When you arrive early, you create space for grace.
You breathe before the world begins.
You listen before you speak.
You prepare before you perform.

It's a quiet declaration of intention:
"I am ready. I am here. I am honoring what matters."

Arrive early, not just for meetings,
but for the life you're meant to lead.

This is Sovereign Living.

UNPREPARED TO PREPARED

> *"By failing to prepare, you are preparing to fail."*
> ~ Benjamin Franklin

Preparedness isn't just about staying ahead of disaster; it's about living from intention rather than reaction. It is the practice of creating stability, freedom, and confidence for yourself and for everyone whose life intersects with yours.

Being prepared doesn't mean you can control everything. It means you have honored what you can. When life happens, and it will, you meet it with presence instead of panic, calm instead of chaos. Preparedness is not rigidity; it is reverence. It allows you to move through change with grounded confidence rather than resistance.

Preparation is one of the most loving forms of leadership. It communicates care, responsibility, and respect for time, energy, and relationships. Whether in business, family, or personal growth, readiness becomes a silent declaration: I am here, I am steady, and I am capable of holding what comes next.

My Story: Planning as a Love Language

As a working mother of three, preparation became my superpower. Not because I loved schedules or color-coded charts, but because I loved my children and wanted to be present with them, not scrambling around them.

Our family calendar lived on the kitchen counter. It was our north star: school dates, sports, holidays, and breaks were all planned with care. Travel was mapped months in advance. And yes, I learned the passport expiration rule the hard way once. Each child had their annual physical in their birthday month, a tradition that began out of practicality but grew into something more. After every appointment, we would stop for ice cream. It was never about the exam; it was about time together, just us.

Dental visits were another act of strategy. All three children had back-to-back appointments after school. It was a logistical miracle, but it saved hours of chaos. When it came to extracurriculars, I treated registration like a concert ticket drop: first come, first served. Delaying meant disappointment. My children's interests were not an afterthought; they were honored in action.

The most emotional chapter, however, was college preparation, not because of essays or applications, but because it marked the beginning of goodbye. So I started planning early with my youngest daughter. Freshman year, we talked about possibilities. Sophomore year, she explored interests. Junior year, a college prep coach helped with timelines and essays. Senior year, she applied early to avoid chaos and panic.

I wanted those final months before she left home to be sacred, not consumed by stress. Preparation was not just for her; it was for me too. Because nothing interrupts connection like last-minute frenzy. Being prepared gave us the gift of presence, the rare, golden kind that lingers long after the moment ends.

Preparation to Demonstrate You Are Protecting What Matters

Preparation is often misunderstood as rigidity or control; but at its core, it's an expression of care. When you take time to plan ahead, you're not just being efficient; you're showing that what (and who) matters to you is worth honoring. Preparation protects your peace, preserves your energy, and creates the spaciousness needed to show up with presence, not panic.

Reflect

Reflection invites you to examine where a lack of preparation might be costing you more than you realize. "Winging it" may seem harmless in the moment, but over time, it can lead to burnout, miscommunication, and unnecessary stress. Acknowledging this without judgment opens the door to greater alignment and peace.

- Where in your life are you consistently "winging it" and what is the emotional, relational, or financial impact of that habit?

- Think of a recent situation where better preparation could have created ease, joy, or deeper connection. What did you learn?

- Who in your life benefits from your readiness? Whether it's children, colleagues, clients, or even your future self, be prepared.

Journaling Prompt: *What would it look like to treat preparation not as pressure, but as protection for what I value most?*

Reframe

Reframing allows you to shift the story you tell yourself about preparation. It's not about controlling every outcome; it's about creating space for presence and adaptability. When you prepare well, you're not being rigid, you're being reverent. You're saying, "This matters. I'm here for it."

- Preparation is not perfectionism. It's an act of devotion to what matters most.
- The more grounded your structure, the more spacious your presence becomes.
- Thoughtful planning is not control, it's compassion for yourself and those who depend on you.

Mantra: *My preparation is a sacred act. It makes room for presence, peace, and purpose.*

Reconnect

Reconnection is about weaving preparation into your daily rhythms with intention and love. By creating systems and structure, you free up energy for creativity, joy, and deeper relationships. Preparation becomes less about "getting ahead" and more about staying rooted in what matters.

- **Create or Update a Shared Family Calendar**
  Include school, sports, travel, meals, and personal goals. Visibility reduces stress and fosters teamwork.

- **Design a Simple Prep Zone**
  Set up a drawer, basket, or shelf for daily grab-and-go items such as car keys, water bottles, chargers, or notes.

- **Try the "Two Is One, One Is None" Principle**
  Restock pantry items, toiletries, and household basics *before* you run out. It builds margin and minimizes stress.

- **Streamline One Area This Week**
  Focus on mornings, meals, or meetings. Notice how intentional preparation shifts your energy and your presence.

Affirmation: *I prepare with love, plan with purpose, and protect what matters most through presence and care.*

Final Thought: Preparation Is a Form of Love

To be prepared is not to be rigid.
It's to honor what matters before the moment arrives.

It's a quiet gesture that whispers,
"I thought of this before you had to."
"I made space for peace."
"I showed up, not by accident, but by design."

Preparedness is not about perfection.
It's about presence.
It's about leading with integrity and heart.

When you prepare with care, you create calm.
You replace chaos with clarity.
You turn pressure into purpose.

Because when others feel your steadiness,
they trust your leadership.
And when you feel your own steadiness,
you trust yourself.

This is Sovereign Living.

DISCIPLINED TO DEVOTIONAL

"People think I am disciplined. It is not discipline. It is devotion. There is a great difference."
~ *Luciano Pavarotti*

Discipline is the backbone of achievement. It brings order, builds habits, and helps us meet life with structure and steadiness. But structure alone can sometimes feel sterile or hollow when disconnected from the heart.

There is a softer, more radiant layer we can choose to bring into our routines: devotion. Devotion transforms duty into desire, and repetition into reverence. It invites meaning into the mundane. Where discipline brings control, devotion brings connection to ourselves, our purpose, and the present moment.

It is not about doing more. It is about being more: more aware, more grateful, more intentional. When discipline becomes devotion, even ordinary acts begin to hum with quiet holiness. It is where mastery meets mindfulness, and where life becomes sacred by design.

My Story: Sacredness in Simple Acts

For me, laundry is not just a chore; it is a practice. Each step is intentional. I sort carefully: whites, colors, delicates. I pre-treat stains with laser focused attention, measuring detergent like a sacred offering and adding a touch of OxiClean as though blessing and purifying the water.

Folding becomes a meditative act: aligning seams, smoothing fabric, and stacking colors in gradients that calm my spirit. My drawers are artfully arranged: solids on the left, patterns on the right, whites curated like a gallery of light. To some, it may look obsessive, but to me, it is devotional. I am not simply caring for clothes; I am honoring the energy and effort that brought them into my life, the body that wears them, and the quiet dignity of tending to what sustains me.

This same reverence began to reshape even the most ordinary routines. Take brushing your teeth. It is basic, essential, often rushed. But when I slowed down, even those two minutes, morning and night, became moments of presence and peace. As I brushed, I began to breathe deeply, speak affirmations, and imagine rinsing away not only plaque but also any harsh words or lingering frustrations.

Over time, I brought that same rhythm into washing dishes, making my bed, and watering plants. Each act became a meditation, a humble ritual of gratitude for the privilege of daily life. Slowly, I noticed something shift the tone of my voice, the way I greeted the day, the softness in how I spoke to others, and even myself.

That is what devotion does. It softens us. It grounds us. And it transforms the ordinary into something quietly extraordinary.

Cultivating Devotion in the Mundane

Devotion isn't limited to spiritual rituals or grand gestures; it lives in how you move through your day. When you infuse ordinary tasks with presence, care, and gratitude, they become sacred. Cultivating devotion in the daily doesn't require more time; it requires more intention. This chapter is an invitation to reclaim your routines as rituals, not for performance, but for peace.

Reflect

Reflection brings awareness to how you move through the patterns of your day. Rushing through tasks may get things done, but often at the expense of your presence. When you bring mindfulness to the ordinary, you remember that your energy, not the task itself, is what gives your life meaning.

- What parts of your daily routine feel mechanical, rushed, or emotionally empty?
- How do you typically relate to discipline? Do you react with resistance, resentment, or quiet pride?
- When was the last time you felt joy or reverence while doing something simple like making tea, folding clothes, or walking outside?

Journaling Prompt: *What is one routine I've overlooked that could become a moment of presence and devotion?*

Reframe

Reframing shifts the meaning of daily responsibilities from obligation to opportunity. Discipline builds the container, but devotion fills it with heart. You don't need a different life to feel connected; you need a different relationship with the life you already live.

- Discipline creates structure and devotion brings it to life.
- Your ordinary tasks can become acts of care, love,

and grounding when done with presence.

- When you bring reverence to what you touch, you amplify its meaning and your own peace.

Mantra: *What I tend to with care, I turn into devotion.*

Reconnect

Reconnection is about weaving reverence into the fabric of your routines. This isn't about slowing everything down; it's about becoming aware, even for a few moments, of the sacred within the simple. When you treat your daily actions as invitations to presence, they stop feeling like chores and start feeling like offerings.

- **Choose One Daily Task to Devote Yourself To**
  Pick something you do often such as making the bed, brushing your teeth, cooking a meal, and thoughtfully bring intention to it.

- **Add Breath, Prayer, or Mantra**
  As you move, repeat quietly:
  – "I honor this body."
  – "I offer this moment to peace."
  – "I move with love."

- **Let Gratitude Infuse the Ordinary**
  As you wash dishes, sweep the floor, or prepare food, silently thank what supports you. Let that shift your energy.

- **Allow Devotion to Expand**
  One mindful act can change the tone of your whole day. Let it ripple, task to task, breath to breath.

Affirmation: *I bring love into the ordinary. My presence turns routine into ritual and action into devotion.*

Final Thought: Let Devotion Be Your Daily Offering

Discipline is admirable.
But devotion is transcendent.

Devotion whispers, *"This moment matters."*
It invites the sacred into the simple.
It infuses ordinary tasks with love,
intention, and soul.

You don't need more hours in the day.
You need more presence in the hours
you already have.

Devotion transforms duty into delight.
It turns repetition into ritual.
It elevates the mundane into the miraculous.

So fold with love.
Brush with purpose.
Breathe with reverence.

Let your daily life become a living prayer,
not of perfection, but of presence.

This is Sovereign Living.

BUYING A GIFT TO THOUGHTFUL GIFT GIVING

"It is not the gift, but the thought that counts."
~ Henry Jackson van Dyke Jr.

In a world of wish lists, shipping deadlines, and same-day delivery, it is easy to forget the heart of true gift giving: thoughtfulness. A meaningful gift is never about price, trend, or convenience. It is about presence, the art of seeing someone clearly and offering something that mirrors their essence back to them.

True giving begins with listening. Not only to words, but to energy, to longing, to the quiet pauses that reveal what someone truly values. The most powerful gifts are rarely extravagant; they are intentional. They carry stories, memories, and emotion. A handwritten note, a framed photograph, or a carefully curated playlist can speak louder than anything store-bought, whispering, "I know you. I see you. I remember what moves you."

The best gifts do not say, "I saw this online." They say, "I see you." They say, "I honor your journey." They say, "You matter." In this way, gift giving becomes a sacred act, a reflection of love translated through attention, presence, and the quiet joy of giving from the soul.

My Story: Legacy Told in Loving Pages

For my mother's seventieth birthday, there were no balloons, no party, and no champagne toast. She had just retired and survived a harrowing battle with stage four colon cancer. She wanted no grand celebration, only quiet, stillness, and reflection.

But the rest of us, her children, grandchildren, brother, in-laws, nieces, and nephews, could not let the moment pass unnoticed. We had almost lost her, and the miracle of her presence demanded to be honored. So instead of a party, I created something gentler, something meant to last far beyond the day itself.

I reached out to her closest circle and invited them to share their favorite memories, their deepest gratitude, and the photographs that captured her essence. What came back was extraordinary: stories spanning decades, handwritten letters, family anecdotes, inside jokes, and prayers of appreciation. Each contribution revealed another layer of her life, painting a portrait of the woman behind the roles; not just "Mom" or "Gma," but friend, mentor, confidante, and quiet matriarch.

I gathered every story into a custom book, not a scrapbook, but a sacred artifact. It was literally a timeline of love and devotion. When she opened it, something softened in her eyes. She read each page slowly, tracing her own story through the words of those she had nurtured, guided, and loved into becoming.

Later, she whispered, "I had no idea that I meant this much to so many." In that moment, I saw her reclaim her worth. The book became more than a gift; it was a mirror of her impact, a vessel of gratitude, and proof that love, when gathered and given back, can heal what words alone cannot.

That is the true purpose of a gift: to reflect someone's light back to them, clearly and tenderly, so its warmth continues to shine long after the moment has passed.

The Power of Thoughtful Giving

To be seen is one of the deepest human desires and one of the most lasting gifts you can offer. Thoughtful giving isn't about price or presentation; it's about presence, attention, and sincerity. When you gift with intention, you create a moment that says: "You matter. I know you. I see who you are." This chapter is an invitation to make giving a sacred act of connection, not through extravagance, but through meaning.

Reflect

Reflection allows you to recall the gifts that left a mark; not because of what they were, but because of how they made you feel. True giving begins with noticing. It's about paying attention to what lights someone up, what they long for, or what they quietly treasure. From that space, you create connection that lasts far beyond the moment.

- What's the most meaningful gift you've ever received and what made it so special?
- Think of someone you'll be giving to soon. What do you admire about them? What do they value deeply?
- When was the last time a gift, big or small, made you feel profoundly seen?

Journaling Prompt: *What would it look like to give not just a thing, but a message: I see you. I understand you. I honor you?*

Reframe

Reframing invites you to shift your perspective from giving as obligation to giving as a gesture of love. The most treasured gifts are often simple, unexpected, and deeply personal. The magic lies not in the cost, but in the care behind it.

- Giving meaningfully isn't about money, it's about mindful presence.
- The best gifts speak to the heart: "I see what lights you up. I thought of you."
- You don't need extravagance to make an impact. You need to pay attention.

Mantra: *I give with presence, not pressure. My attention is the most valuable gift I offer.*

Reconnect

Reconnection is the practice of turning giving into a consistent expression of love and attentiveness. By listening closely, collecting small details, and offering thoughtful gestures, you transform everyday interactions into lasting memories. When you give with intention, you offer someone the most sacred gift: being seen.

- **Create a Gift Notes Section on Your Phone**
  When someone mentions a favorite book, memory, dream, or wish, jot it down. Let everyday conversations inspire future gifts.

- **Use Storytelling for Milestones**
  For birthdays, anniversaries, or farewells, gather stories, letters, or photos from others. Give the gift of collective memory and meaning.

- **Practice Everyday Gifting**
  A handwritten note. A single flower from your garden. A playlist that reminds you of them. Let your gifts reflect care, not cost.
- **Let Your Gifts Speak Clearly**
  Use your gift to say what matters:
  – You matter.
  – I see you.
  – I care.

Affirmation: *I give with presence, honor with intention, and create connection through the gift of being fully seen.*

Final Thought: Let Your Gifts Tell a Love Story

A true gift is never about the thing;
it's about the message.

It says: *I've been paying attention.*
It says: *You are important to me.*
It says: *Your presence in my life is worth celebrating.*

Whether it's a handmade card,
a shared experience,
or a well-chosen item wrapped with care,
let your gifts become love letters.

Not just for birthdays or holidays,
but for the quiet, ordinary days that shape a life.

When you give with thoughtfulness,
you give something far more valuable than any object.
You give meaning.
You give memory.
You give magic.

This is Sovereign Living.

TEXT OR EMAIL TO HANDWRITTEN NOTE

"Using thank you notes strengthens the bond between people in your personal life and in business. They ring an emotional chord."
~ Cristiano Magni

When was the last time you received a handwritten thank-you note? Not a thumbs-up emoji. Not a quick "thx" in a text. But an envelope. Ink. Someone's time. There is a kind of intimacy in seeing another person's handwriting: imperfect, human, and real. In that moment, connection becomes tangible, and gratitude turns into art.

In a fast-paced world ruled by screens, the simple act of writing by hand has become a quiet devotion. It slows time. It captures presence. It anchors emotion in something lasting. A handwritten note transforms a fleeting feeling into something you can hold, reread, and cherish long after digital words have disappeared into the endless scroll. It becomes a sacred pause in an otherwise hurried world.

A handwritten note does more than say "thank you." It says, "You mattered enough for me to stop and reflect". It says, "I value you, not just for what you did but for who you are." It is an act of care that bridges distance and deepens trust. Long after the ink has dried, the energy remains as a small gesture that leaves a lasting impression and a timeless reminder that sincerity never goes out of style.

My Story: Notes That Bridge Hearts

I first fell in love with thank-you notes in my early twenties, around the time when bridal showers, weddings, and baby gifts began to fill my calendar.

Each time I received a card in return, I noticed the effort, the emotion, the way someone's handwriting carried personality, care, and warmth. It felt intimate, like a conversation that lived outside of time. Something shifted in me. I began viewing gratitude not just as a sentiment, but as a spiritual practice, a ritual that built bridges between hearts.

When I became a mother, I wanted my children to learn this same practice. Before they could even write, we found ways for them to participate: thumbprints, little scribbles, watercolor swirls inside the card. I remember a school fundraiser where my youngest daughter's tiny handprint was captured on notecards. We used those for her birthday thank-yous that year, her "signature" already beginning to leave a trail of appreciation.

As they grew older, I encouraged them to write their own notes, not out of politeness but presence. To take a few moments to think about the person, the moment, and the gift. Today, I still send handwritten notes to family, friends, and colleagues not just for gifts, but for kindnesses, for time shared, for being who they are.

Because every note is more than ink on paper. It is a whisper of connection, a gesture of remembrance, a tangible echo of love made visible. Gratitude, when given form, becomes sacred. It travels farther than the page, carrying warmth that lingers quietly in the heart, long after the words have faded.

Building Connection through Handwritten Gratitude

In an age of instant messages and digital notifications, the handwritten note has become a quiet act of reverence. To put pen to paper is to slow down, to be intentional, and to make gratitude tangible. A thank-you note doesn't just express appreciation, it creates a lasting imprint of love, recognition, and connection. This chapter is an invitation to return to the art of handwritten gratitude as a sacred and simple way to let others feel seen.

Reflect

Reflection allows you to pause and consider who in your life might need to feel valued and how often we overlook the power of written words. Gratitude doesn't have to be grand; it simply needs to be expressed. Writing it by hand adds a layer of presence that can't be replicated by a screen.

- When was the last time you wrote someone a handwritten note and how did it feel to send or receive it?
- Who in your life could use a reminder that they matter, that they've impacted you, or that they're appreciated?
- Have you ever kept a thank-you card or note? What made it memorable enough to hold onto?

Journaling Prompt: *Who needs to hear my gratitude and what would it mean for me to write it, not just say it?*

Reframe

Reframing helps you recognize that handwritten gratitude isn't outdated, it's deeply meaningful. In a fast-moving world, choosing to slow down and write something by hand is an act of love. Your message doesn't need to be perfect, it just needs to be real.

- A thank-you note isn't old-fashioned; it's timeless. It speaks to the heart, not just the moment.
- Handwritten words have staying power. They are often read, saved, and revisited long after they're received.
- Gratitude is the gift. The card is simply its vessel, a sacred wrapper for something heartfelt and human.

Mantra: *My words matter more when they're offered with presence and care.*

Reconnect

Reconnection is about creating space in your life for intentional expressions of gratitude. It's not about waiting for a perfect moment. It's about choosing to speak love and thanks when it's least expected and most needed. A handwritten note is a way to slow down and let someone know: I see you. I remember. I appreciate you.

- **Keep Gratitude Materials Accessible**
  Set aside a drawer or basket with blank cards, pens, and stamps. Make it easy to act when gratitude stirs in you.

- **Write to Someone Today**
  Choose one person. It could be a mentor, friend, sibling, teacher, or a child. Keep it simple. Let your sincerity lead.

- **Celebrate the Everyday**
  Don't wait for a promotion, birthday, or big gesture. Thank someone for showing up, for listening, for just being who they are.

- **Let Your Handwriting Be Enough**
  Your note doesn't need to be eloquent. It needs to be yours. Messy, emotional, heartfelt and that's the magic.

Affirmation: *I write with presence. My words carry love, and my gratitude becomes connection that lasts.*

Final Thought: Let Gratitude Leave a Trace

A handwritten note is a love letter
to the present moment.
It says: *You mattered to me.*
Enough to slow down.
Enough to say thank you with care.

In a world of fast reactions,
be the one who offers reflection.
In a culture of noise,
be the whisper of sincerity.

Because words written by hand
carry more than ink,
they carry presence, intention, and soul.

Gratitude that lives on paper
becomes a keepsake of kindness,
a tangible reminder of connection.

Leave traces of appreciation wherever you go.
Let your thank-yous become timeless.

This is Sovereign Living.

SORRY TO EXCUSE ME

"No. You never apologize for something you didn't do wrong. You say 'excuse me.' Never 'I'm sorry.' If you spend your life apologizing, you'll never gain any confidence."

~ *J.T. Ellison*

"Sorry" is a word we learn early to be polite, to ease discomfort, to smooth what feels uneasy. Yet over time, and especially for women, that small word can grow heavy. It becomes less about kindness and more about conditioning, a subtle script that teaches us to take up less space in the world.

We say sorry when we enter a room, when someone else bumps into us, when we ask for what we need. We apologize for our emotions, our boundaries, even our brilliance. Sometimes, we whisper sorry for simply existing too loudly. Each unnecessary apology chips away at our confidence, dulling the truth of who we are.

But what if the goal isn't to be sorry? What if the goal is to be awake and to meet each moment with awareness, compassion, and self-respect? Presence does not require apology. It asks only that we stay grounded enough to speak truth with grace, even when it feels uncomfortable.

There is a quiet power in shifting from "I'm sorry" to "Excuse me." The first absorbs blame; the second honors boundaries, both ours and others. This simple change in language reshapes posture, energy, and self-worth. Learning that distinction is how we begin to reclaim confidence, clarity, and the calm authority of our own voice.

My Story: Beyond Sorry, Toward Truth

I was a chronic over-apologizer. "Sorry" slipped out of my mouth before I even realized why I was saying it. It appeared in texts, emails, and conversations, almost like punctuation.

During my divorce, that habit took center stage. Every time I stood in front of my soon-to-be ex-husband or looked into my children's tearful eyes, "I'm sorry" was all I could offer. I wasn't sorry for ending the marriage; I knew it was necessary. But I was sorry for the pain it caused, sorry for the confusion, sorry that they didn't yet understand, sorry that I didn't have the perfect words. It became a loop. I'm sorry, I'm sorry, I'm sorry.

One day, in a counseling session designed to help my son process his emotions, he was asked to choose an object from the room to represent each family member. For me, he chose the board game *Sorry!* The therapist gently explained his choice: "My mom is so sorry for what's happening." I felt the truth land in my chest like a thunderclap. He didn't see me as a safe, grounded mother. He saw me as someone stuck in remorse, unable to lead.

That moment changed me. I realized my constant apologizing was not helping him or me. My son was young, tender, and deeply hurt, and no amount of explanation could reach him then. My words of regret, spoken from love, landed instead as reminders of pain. He could not yet separate my sorrow from his own. And I don't blame him. He was a young teenager, trying to make sense of a world that had suddenly shifted beneath him.

For years, I carried that ache; the distance between what I meant to convey and what he could receive. Healing took time, patience, and faith. There were long stretches of silence, moments of misunderstanding, and quiet prayers whispered into the dark. Yet beneath it all, love remained steady, waiting for the right season to be heard.

When the time finally came, our conversations changed. They grew softer, steadier, and more grounded. I began to speak differently. I said things like, "Please forgive me for the pain this transition caused." "Please know this choice came from a place of deep reflection, even if it didn't feel good at the time."

Those words were not easy, but they were true. Over the years, through honesty and grace, we found our way back to understanding. I learned that sometimes love cannot be heard in the moment; it must be lived into being. The most healing words are not always "I'm sorry," but "I see you." They are "I understand this is hard." They are "I'm here, and I'm still standing in love with you."

Transforming Sorry to an Honest Acknowledgment

Apologies should not shrink us; they should free us. Saying "I'm sorry" is a sacred act when it is sincere, specific, and rooted in growth. But when we apologize reflexively, we trade truth for approval and peace for guilt.

This chapter invites you to transform over-apologizing into empowered acknowledgment: to speak truth with tenderness, to repair without self-erasure, and to let compassion replace contrition. True apology is not about guilt; it is about growth, grace, and grounded self-respect.

Reflect

Reflection invites you to become aware of your patterns with apologies. Are you saying "I'm sorry" to maintain peace, avoid tension, or soften your presence? When apologies are misused, they chip away at your voice and worth. Honest acknowledgment, on the other hand, builds trust with others and with yourself.

- Do you find yourself apologizing when you're simply expressing a need or taking up space?
- What kinds of situations trigger you to say "I'm sorry" even when no harm has been done?
- When was the last time you apologized and felt yourself shrink instead of feel seen?

Journaling Prompt: *Where have I used "I'm sorry" to shrink myself, and what could I say instead that honors both truth and dignity?*

Reframe

Reframing helps you understand that apologies are most powerful when they are precise and rooted in integrity. You can take responsibility for your impact without collapsing into guilt. Sometimes, what's really needed is gratitude, clarity, or presence, not shame.

- "I'm sorry" isn't always the most accurate or empowering response.
- Consider alternatives: "Thank you for your patience." "I see how that affected you." "Please excuse the delay."
- You can acknowledge hurt or missteps without confusing your actions with your identity.

Mantra: *I own my impact with clarity and care, not with shame or self-erasure.*

Reconnect

Reconnection is about repairing with honesty and honoring yourself in the process. Whether you're making amends to someone else or to yourself, the goal isn't perfection; it's presence. Clear language and sincere accountability heal far more than empty apologies.

- **Pause Before You Apologize**
  Ask yourself: "What am I really feeling?" "What am I trying to restore?" "Is it peace, connection, or control?"

- **Make Repairs with Precision**
  If harm was done, say: "Please forgive me for…" and name the action. Avoid labeling yourself as bad; instead, name what happened and how you'll do better.

- **Practice Self-Forgiveness**
  Write a note or speak aloud: "I forgive myself for…" and name what you've carried too long. Let go of shame. Keep the lesson.

- **Model Empowered Language**
  Teach your children, peers, and loved ones what true ownership sounds like. Let them see what accountability looks like when paired with self-respect.

Affirmation: *I speak truth without shrinking. I repair with care and stand in my worth with clarity and grace.*

Final Thought: Speak from Your Power, Not Your Pain

"I'm sorry" has its place,
but it should never be the anthem of your worth.

When you replace over-apologizing
with clear, loving accountability,
you reclaim your voice.

You stand in truth without self-abandonment.
You model grace without groveling.
You honor what is yours to carry
and release what is not.

Let your words reflect who you truly are:
Aware. Evolving. Empowered.

Apology when needed.
Authenticity always.

This is how you lead with self-respect.
This is how you teach others to meet you
with the same.

This is Sovereign Living.

APOLOGY TO APPRECIATION

*"An apology is a lovely perfume;
it can transform the clumsiest
moment into a gracious gift."*
~ Margaret Lee Runbeck

This practice builds naturally upon the previous chapter **Sorry to Excuse Me**, inviting us to go even deeper, to take moments of discomfort or misstep and turn them into gestures of grace. Rather than centering on fault or guilt, this shift invites us to elevate connection, awareness, and gratitude in real time.

Imagine arriving late to a meeting. Instead of blurting, "Sorry I'm late," you pause, take a breath, and say, "Thank you for waiting for me." The energy changes immediately. One centers on what went wrong; the other acknowledges care, patience, and respect.

When we replace apology with appreciation, we do not dismiss accountability; we transform it. Gratitude softens edges and opens hearts. What could have been a moment of awkwardness becomes an opportunity to build trust, communicate presence, and honor the humanity in both yourself and the other person.

My Story: Communication Rooted in Respect

In real estate, communication is not just a professional courtesy; it is sacred. Especially during escrow, when timelines tighten and emotions can run high, clarity and responsiveness sustain confidence. A single delay can ripple into tension, so every exchange matters.

During one recent transaction with a 21-day close, I was managing an intense pace of emails, calls, inspections, and negotiations. By the end of the week, I felt my energy thinning. On Saturday evening, I allowed myself a rare pause: one hour for a yoga class. I left my phone in the car and gave myself permission to breathe.

When I returned to my messages, I noticed a note from my client. It wasn't urgent; it was simply a clarifying question about an inspection detail. My instinct was to type, "Sorry for the delay," but I caught myself. Instead, I wrote, "Hi [Client], please excuse my delayed response. Thank you for your patience."

His reply was immediate: "No worries at all. I hope you're doing something fun." The energy was different: light, kind, and balanced. There was no guilt, no friction. Just mutual respect.

That small moment reminded me how language shapes energy. By choosing appreciation over apology, I preserved the warmth of the relationship and modeled the calm I wanted reflected back. It was a simple shift, but it carried weight. It served as a reminder that grace in communication begins with presence, not perfection.

Replacing Guilt with Gratitude

Many of us use "sorry" as a default, a filler, a softener, or a shield. But when no harm has been done, this habit can erode our confidence and create disconnection. Presence doesn't require an apology. It requires sincerity. This chapter invites you to replace automatic guilt with conscious gratitude, transforming everyday exchanges into moments of empowered connection.

Reflect

Reflection invites you to notice the ways you offer apologies when what's truly needed is presence or appreciation. Over-apologizing can subtly signal self-doubt or disrupt healthy communication. Recognizing these patterns is the first step in reclaiming your voice and offering others the energy of grounded presence.

- Do you say "sorry" out of habit, even when no harm occurred?

- Have you experienced the difference when someone responds with appreciation instead of apology? How did it feel?

- What common moments in your life could be softened, healed, or empowered by simply shifting the language you use?

Journaling Prompt: *Where have I been apologizing for my presence and how can I shift toward offering appreciation instead?*

Reframe

Reframing helps you see that "sorry" isn't always the most honest or helpful response. Often, we say it to manage discomfort, rather than to express care. By flipping "sorry" into "thank you," you shift the tone of the interaction from guilt to grace, and from self-erasure to mutual respect.

- "Sorry" can be a stand-in for discomfort. Appreciation communicates presence with perspective.

- You don't need to carry guilt to show care. You can stay connected without self-minimizing.

- Saying "thank you" invites grace, acknowledges effort, and deepens trust.

Mantra: *I choose gratitude over guilt. My presence is enough.*

Reconnect

Reconnection is about using your words to reflect clarity, confidence, and care. In small, everyday moments, especially when tension is low but uncertainty is high, choosing appreciation over apology creates a bridge. When your language affirms connection instead of questioning it, you reinforce your value and invite others to do the same.

- **Practice Flipping Common Phrases**
  – *"Sorry I asked again."* to *"Thank you for your patience."*
  – *"Sorry to bring this up."* to *"Thank you for being open to the conversation."*

- **Pause Before You Apologize**
  Ask yourself: "What am I truly trying to express?" "Is this an apology or a need for acknowledgment, clarity, or care?"

- **Let Appreciation Be Your Default**
  Especially in moments of small tension, lead with "thank you" instead of "sorry." Gratitude softens the moment without sacrificing your voice.

- **Choose Presence, Not Performance**
  You don't need to make yourself smaller to be kind. Your words can reflect both humility and confidence.

Affirmation: *I offer presence, not apology. I lead with appreciation, grounded in worth and grace.*

Final Thought: Turn Guilt into Grace

Appreciation is a soft superpower.
It disarms defensiveness.
It dissolves awkwardness.
It strengthens connection.

When you say "thank you" instead of "I'm sorry,"
you shift the energy
from guilt to grace,
from shame to shared humanity.

Let your language reflect your values:
Connection over perfection.
Gratitude over guilt.
Presence over performance.

You're not here to apologize for your existence.
You're here to honor the people, the moments, the energy around you with warmth,
with awareness, with respect.

This is Sovereign Living.

EATING TO DINING

*"Manners are a sensitive awareness
of the feelings of others.
If you have that awareness,
you have good manners,
no matter what fork you use."*
~ *Emily Post*

Dining is not simply the act of eating, it is the art of honoring nourishment. It's where gratitude meets grace, where conversation becomes communion, and where presence turns an ordinary meal into a sacred ritual of connection.

In a world of rushing, scrolling, and multitasking, we often forget that sharing a meal is one of humanity's oldest expressions of respect for food, for others, and for ourselves. True dining invites us to slow down, engage all our senses, and meet one another in awareness.

The essence of etiquette at the table is not perfection, it's mindfulness. It's how we bring reverence to the simple act of eating, transforming it into an experience of elegance and ease.

My Story: Transforming a Meal into a Moment of Mindful Grace

My favorite meals have always been those shared during the holidays: Thanksgiving, Christmas Eve, Christmas Day, New Year's Eve, and New Year's Day. Each is a collective act of love, orchestrated by the host who crafts the menu and invites others to contribute their talents. The table becomes a tapestry of effort and care, each dish a reflection of someone's devotion.

My favorite moment comes just before the meal begins, when the kitchen hums with anticipation, every dish timed perfectly, the air fragrant with promise, and the dining room filling with laughter and the gentle rhythm of gathering. Guests choose their seats, settling into what will become hours of communion, eating, drinking, and sharing stories that linger long after the plates are cleared.

In our family, the women instinctively rise to assist the host, ensuring every final detail is touched with grace. The flowers are arranged, the tablecloth smoothed, and the colors harmonized. Before eating, we join hands in prayer, each offering words of gratitude. Sometimes laughter fills the space; other times, tears fall as we remember those no longer with us. Even the children have learned to listen deeply, and to express their hearts with sincerity and respect.

Phones are never allowed at the table, except perhaps for a single photo capturing the beauty of the spread and the faces gathered around it. After the meal, we linger. No one rushes to clear plates. The food remains, a quiet invitation to savor seconds or nibble on favorites that appear only once a year.

The food is always delicious, but it is the *conversation* that nourishes most. The pace is unhurried, the air filled with gratitude, the moment suspended in grace. For me, it is not the menu that matters most, but the mindfulness and the slow rhythm of togetherness that turns a simple meal into a sacred memory.

Below are timeless dining principles from Emily Post, whose wisdom on etiquette reminds us that small, intentional gestures create ease, presence, and harmony at every table:

- **Chew with your mouth closed.** Respect begins with discretion; it allows conversation, not consumption, to take center stage.

- **Keep your smartphone off the table and silenced.** The people before you deserve your undivided attention. Presence is the most refined form of courtesy.

- **Hold utensils correctly.** They are extensions of your intention and instruments of grace, not tools of haste.

- **Arrive clean and composed.** Wash up before the meal; the table is for nourishment, not grooming.

- **Use your napkin thoughtfully.** It is a quiet act of self-respect and care for those dining with you.

- **Wait to sip until you've finished chewing.** It's a pause of patience that keeps the moment fluid and graceful.

- **Match your pace to your companions.** Dining is a shared rhythm; harmony at the table mirrors harmony in life.

- **Mind your posture.** Sit upright, with ease and confidence. Elbows may rest gently between courses. A gentle reminder that etiquette is flexible, not rigid.

- **Ask for what you need.** Instead of reaching, invite connection: "Would you please pass the bread?" Every request becomes an opportunity for warmth.

- **Bring your best self to the meal.** Engage in conversation. Listen deeply. Laughter, curiosity, and gratitude season the table more richly than any spice.

The Sacred Art of Dining

Dining is one of the oldest rituals of connection, a sacred act that reminds us to slow down, to listen, and to honor the moment we share with others. It is less about polished performance and more about energetic presence, how you make others feel, how you receive what is offered, and how you express gratitude through grace.

When approached with intention, dining becomes an expression of mindfulness, a mirror of how you engage with life itself. To dine is to practice elegance of spirit: to eat with awareness, to converse with kindness, and to let your presence nourish the room as much as the meal.

Reflect

Reflection invites you to see dining as a sacred mirror, one that reflects your relationship with nourishment, self-worth, and connection. The table is not a stage; it is a sanctuary. Notice the energy you bring to it. Are you rushed or receptive, distracted or present, self-conscious or serene? Dining with grace begins with awareness of how you show up.

Ask yourself:

- "How do I approach the table?" "Am I hurried, hungry, or grateful?"
- "What emotions arise when I dine with others?"
- "Do I savor my food and conversation, or do I rush through both?"
- "How can I transform an ordinary meal into a mindful ritual of appreciation?"

Journal Prompt: *Describe a meal that felt truly nourishing, not just to your body, but to your spirit. What made it meaningful? Who were you being in that moment?*

Reframe

Reframing helps you remember that dining is not about perfection, but presence. You are not performing etiquette; you are embodying grace. The rules of refinement were never meant to restrict; they were created to harmonize, to help you move through shared space with ease and respect. When you eat with awareness, you transform a simple act into an art form. a meditation of movement, breath, and gratitude.

- Every gesture, passing a dish, lifting a glass, saying thank you, is a chance to communicate respect.
- Your presence at the table is your offering. Your energy sets the tone.
- The real beauty of etiquette is not in how you hold your fork, but in how you hold space.

Mantra: *I bring mindfulness to every meal, allowing grace to flow through my presence.*

Reconnect

Reconnection is the practice of returning to the table, not just to eat, but to belong. When you dine consciously, you create community. When you listen deeply, you create trust. When you express gratitude, you invite grace to stay.

- **Make dining a devotional act**
  Light a candle, pause before your first bite, or share one word of gratitude aloud. Let every meal remind you that nourishment is sacred and that connection begins with presence.

- **Set the Scene**
  Create a welcoming space: clear the table, add flowers, soften the light.

- **Unplug**
  Keep your phone out of sight; make eye contact with the people in front of you.

- **Savor**
  Eat slowly, notice textures and flavors, and breathe between bites.

- **Give Thanks**
  A quiet word of gratitude transforms eating into communion.

Affirmation: *I honor the table as sacred ground. I eat with gratitude, speak with grace, and allow my presence to nourish every soul I share a meal with.*

Final Thought: Dining as Devotion

To dine is to honor the sacred in the ordinary.
It is to pause long enough to feel gratitude
before the first bite.
It is to recognize that nourishment
is not just for the body, but for the heart,
the spirit, the connection between souls.

When you eat with grace,
you transform routine into ritual.
When you listen with presence,
you turn conversation into communion.
The table becomes a sanctuary,
and every gesture a prayer.

There is no performance here; only presence.
No perfection; only awareness.
Dining, at its highest form, is an act of love.

So light the candle.
Pass the bread.
Offer your smile as the first course.
Let gratitude be the wine that fills every cup.

This is Sovereign Living.

Pro Tip:

Wait for all table guests, including the host, before putting a morsel of food in your mouth.

ACKNOWLEDGEMENTS

I'd like to acknowledge the many teachers I've met along the way, around the globe:

Soul Sisters
Kimberly Konstant, Business and Soulbbatical Travel Partner
Lisa Tenore, Yoga Teacher and Divinely Guided Intuitive

Book Co-Creation
Helane Freeman, Design & Layout
Mitch Sisskind, Editor
Sydney Koenig, Photography

Yoga-Mindful Teachers
Alexia Daksha Damini, Alice Khalsa, Bilge Alpay, Carla Fabre, Chrissy MJ Anderson, Christopher Tompkins, Colleen Lila Yoga, Elana Brower, Guru Jagat, Guru Jas Khalsa, Harijiwan, Harmanjot Kaur, Isa Raim, Parashakti, Philipp Manser, Ram Kirin, Raquel Griffin, Sarah Miller: Siri Akasha, Schuyler Grant, Shiva Rea, Susan Shaner, Teddy Dean, Tej Kaur Khalsa

Guides
Agus Sihman, Ama, Andrea Caresse, Ellen Goldberg, Ingo Alexander Sohn, Janet Schmidt, Jessica Kruskamp, June Fagan, Krista Polinsky, Nicole Rager, Saul, Taita, Tracy Mignon

Thought Leaders & Book Authors
Alan Watts, Barbara Waxman, Brene Brown, Bruce Feiler, Bruce Lipton, Carol Dweck, Chip Conley, Crystal and Mark Victor Hansen, Danielle LaPorte, David Kessler, Deepak Chopra,

Dr. Gabor Maté, Dr. Gary Chapman,
Don Miguel Ruiz, Eckhart Tolle, Elizabeth Gilbert,
Esther Perel, Gabrielle Bernstein, Gregg Braden,
Haamid Dash, Helane Anderson, Iyanla Vanzant,
Jay Rubin, Jay Shetty, Joe Dispenza, John Gray,
Katherine Woodward Thomas,
Leigh and Carla McCloskey, Louise Hay,
Marie Forleo, Mark Nepo, Matthew McConaughey,
Mel Robbins, Michaela Boehm, Norma Kamali,
Paulo Coelho, Reverend Michael Bernard Beckwith,
Rhonda Byrne, Rich Roll, Rob Bell, Shelley Paxton,
Simon Sinek, Vishen Lakhiani and Wayne Dyer

A heartfelt thank you to **Chip Conley**, founder of Modern Elder Academy, and **Gerard Armond Powell**, founder of Rythmia Life Advancement Center.

In beautifully distinct yet equally transformative ways, you each became luminous guides on my journey toward intentional living. Though your paths differ in form, they meet in purpose: a shared devotion to helping others remember who they are and what they are here to become.

Through my years serving as Marketing Director within both of your worlds, I was given a rare privilege: a front-row seat to transformation in its purest form. Chip, your work at Modern Elder Academy reshaped how I view aging, purpose, and wisdom, revealing that elderhood is not a closing chapter but a profound awakening. Gerry, your vision at Rythmia illuminated the sacred union between healing and wholeness, reminding me that freedom begins when the heart comes home to itself.

Your retreats, your teachings, and your unwavering belief in human potential each invited me into deeper truth. You inspired me to live more consciously, to love more courageously, and to help women everywhere reclaim their Sovereignty, their radiant and unshakable sense of self.

I carry the essence of both of your teachings within my own work, grateful for the intersection of grace, grit, and growth that our paths have shared. May we continue to meet in spaces of awakening, wherever hearts gather to remember the sacred truth of who they are.

ABOUT THE AUTHOR

Laura Alfano is the visionary behind *Sovereign Living*, a movement to inspire 20 million women worldwide to reclaim their Crown, Heart and Compass, and to fully embody their power. Born and raised in Port Chester, New York, as the eldest of three, she grew up rooted in the values of faith, perseverance, and family. A natural achiever, she graduated high school early, earned her associate's degree in Fashion Merchandising, and went on to complete a bachelor's degree in Marketing and Management at Pace University.

After college, Laura married, welcomed three healthy children into the world, and raised them while simultaneously building a successful career in marketing with leading consumer packaged goods companies and creative agencies in the NY/CT area. She later transitioned into consulting to create a healthier balance for her family, carrying her instinct for beauty and design into every role she touched.

In 2007, Laura's life was forever altered by the sudden loss of her brother. What began in heartbreak set off a chain reaction of deeper pain and disappointment: the unraveling of her marriage and the painful estrangement from two of her children. Following her losses, Laura embarked on a spiritual journey of self-discovery, a season of exploration and awakening. As a devoted student, she traveled widely, studied various yoga lineages, read extensively in the fields of personal growth, and participated in transformational courses.

Even an unplanned plant medicine journey became part of her path toward healing. Through this process, Laura reclaimed her Sovereignty, rediscovering her Crown of self-worth, her Heart of compassion, and her Compass of inner wisdom.

Today, Laura lives seaside in Malibu, California, delighting in her role as mother and grandmother. She is a Luxury Real Estate Advisor, a certified Hatha and Kundalini Yoga teacher and Reiki Master. Out of her personal journey, she created the *Sovereign Living* series of books, workbooks, and inspiration cards; resources designed to help women everywhere embody their worth and rise into lives of beauty, balance, joy, and Sovereignty.

DISCOVER THE SOVEREIGN LIVING COLLECTION

Continue your journey of self-discovery and empowerment with the complete *Sovereign Living* series. Alongside each book, you'll find a companion workbook to help you Reflect, Reframe, and Reconnect, plus a deck of inspiration cards to keep your practice alive every day. Choose one or embrace them all to reclaim your Crown, your Heart, and your Compass.

Sovereign Living I: A Woman's Guide to Reclaiming Your Crown

Sovereign Living I Workbook: Reclaiming Your Crown - Reflect, Reframe, Reconnect

Sovereign Living I Inspiration Cards: Reclaiming Your Crown

Sovereign Living II: A Woman's Guide to Reclaiming Your Heart

Sovereign Living II Workbook: Reclaiming Your Heart - Reflect, Reframe, Reconnect

Sovereign Living II Inspiration Cards: Reclaiming Your Heart

Sovereign Living III: A Woman's Guide to Reclaiming Your Compass

Sovereign Living III Workbook: Reclaiming Your Compass - Reflect, Reframe, Reconnect

Sovereign Living III Inspiration Cards: Reclaiming Your Compass

Workbooks and Inspiration Cards coming as soon as 2026